IDIOTS, MADMEN, AND OTHER PRISONERS IN DICKENS

IDIOTS, MADMEN, AND OTHER PRISONERS IN DICKENS

Natalie McKnight

St. Martin's Press
New York

First published in the United States of America 1993

Printed in the United States of America

ISBN 0-312-08596-6

Library of Congress Cataloging-in-Publication Data

McKnight, Natalie.
Idiots, madmen, and other prisoners in Dickens / Natalie McKnight.
        p.   cm.
    Includes bibliographical references and index.
    ISBN 0-312-08596-6
    1. Dickens, Charles, 1812-1870—Characters—Mentally handicapped.
2. Dickens, Charles, 1812-1870—Characters—Mentally ill.
3. Dickens, Charles, 1812-1870—Characters—Prisoners. 4. Mentally
handicapped in literature. 5. Mentally ill in literature.
6. Prisoners in literature. I. Title.

PR4589.M37 1993
823'.8—dc20   92-36304
                                                         CIP

To Jamie and Emily,
my partners in foolishness.

CONTENTS

ACKNOWLEDGMENTS

I would like to thank Michael Cotsell, Fred Kaplan, Jerry Beasley, Carl Dawson, Barbara Gates, and Kevin Kerrane for their helpful comments on earlier drafts of this work. I am also indebted to John Carey, whose Oxford University lectures on Dickens (Michaelmas term, 1982) first sparked my interest in Dickens. The encouragement (and books) he gave me have been a great help. I also owe much to the late Elliot Gilbert, who furthered my interest in and knowledge of Dickens. His Dickens seminar at the University of Delaware was one of the most memorable experiences of my academic career.

I would like to thank the staffs of the libraries at the University of Delaware, Southern Methodist University, the University of Texas at Arlington, Boston University, and the Widener Library at Harvard for their tireless and cheerful service.

Many friends and family members have helped in tangible and intangible ways, and I thank all of them. I am indebted to Judith Allen Ward and Patricia Hock for their friendship, encouragement, and advice. Both were lifelines to me, and I will always be grateful. Marge Betley deserves much thanks for her faith in me and for carefully listening to rather long (and tedious) explanations of Chapters 3 and 4. I also thank Nancy Gillio for her moral support and for offering typesetting assistance.

I am grateful to my colleagues at Boston University for their encouragement. I particularly thank Michael Mahon for sharing drafts of his book on Foucault with me. The clarity and insight of his work was invaluable to me in my own writing.

My brother-in-law, Jonathan McKnight, deserves much thanks for his many offers of assistance. His solutions to the various problems I encountered while writing were always refreshing and liberating.

My parents deserve much gratitude for their faith in me and their interest in my work. In addition, their persistent intellectual curiosity has been an example for me throughout my life. I also thank my brother, Scott Brown, and Elizabeth Gutekunst for moral support and for the many stimulating discussions they have sparked.

Finally, I thank my husband, Jamie McKnight, for reading Dickens and discussing him with me, for giving me a tremendous amount of emotional support, and for creating an environment in which I could create. And I thank my infant phenomenon, Emily, who is always a joy and who fortunately took enough naps so that I could complete this project.

ABBREVIATIONS

AN	*American Notes*
BH	*Bleak House*
BR	*Barnaby Rudge*
CC	*A Christmas Carol*
CS	*Christmas Stories*
DC	*David Copperfield*
D&S	*Dombey and Son*
GE	*Great Expectations*
HT	*Hard Times*
LD	*Little Dorrit*
MC	*Martin Chuzzlewit*
ED	*The Mystery of Edwin Drood*
NN	*Nicholas Nickleby*
OCS	*The Old Curiosity Shop*
OT	*Oliver Twist*
OMF	*Our Mutual Friend*
PP	*The Pickwick Papers*
SB	*Sketches by Boz*
TTC	*A Tale of Two Cities*
UT	*The Uncommercial Traveller*

Chapter 1

Introduction: A World of Private Worlds

Throughout his life, Dickens was fascinated by isolated, imprisoned figures—people trapped in private worlds and private languages. As a boy, he experienced intense periods of isolation that haunted him all his life. As an adult, he made a habit of studying the isolated and imprisoned, in particular inmates of workhouses, prisons, insane asylums, and institutes for the deaf, dumb, and blind. He was moved by the way these people were trapped in extreme states of privacy, often unable to communicate with others at all, and marginalized from the mainstream of society. Dickens recognized isolation as a general human condition, yet he also recognized that for some, isolation was cruelly intensified: the solitary prisoner alone with his guilt and fears; the idiots and madmen adrift in their separate realities; the deaf, dumb, and blind cut off in a dark and silent void. With such fictional and nonfictional characters, characters trapped in physical and or mental prisons, Dickens explores extreme cases of isolation, often criticizing the social practices that create or enhance isolation and marginalization. But his characterizations offer more than just social commentary; they come to represent a philosophy of life, one that is intriguing if not systematic. In this study, I examine first the biographical and social contexts that influence Dickens's portrayals of these figures, then analyze the structural and thematic roles they play in his novels. Throughout, I emphasize and try to account for the strange and compelling vicissitudes in his treatments of idiots, madmen, and other prisoners.[1]

Discussing Dickens's prisoners, idiots, and madmen as a group is not only justified because of their shared experiences of marginalization and imprisonment, but also because Dickens repeats certain images and patterns in their characterizations that suggest he recognized and wished to explore their relation. These images and patterns frequently involve details of clothing, scene, and speech, all of which will be discussed in detail in following chapters.

Another significant similarity that binds these characters together is their use of problematic idiolects, or private languages. All people capable of communication have their own idiolects, but Dickens endows many of his isolated characters with idiolects that are particularly "private" since they overtly block communication. The prefix "idio," which comes from the Greek for "private," emphasizes the connection between idiots and idiolects, but other of Dickens's private characters display particularly isolating idiolects as well. The idiolects of Dickens's idiots, madmen, and other prisoners emphasize their extreme isolation while accentuating their similarities to each other. These private languages are sometimes comic, sometimes so sparse as to render the speaker a near mute, but invariably they help to identify and particularize characters. At the same time, idiolects are a product of isolation and contribute to, sometimes even cause, the alienation of these characters.[2] Occasionally these idiolects are almost incomprehensible, but other times they are simply rejected by more normalized, less marginalized speakers because of prejudice. One must speak the language of the realm to be accepted by it; Dickens's prisoners of private worlds, therefore, are often not accepted. Consequently, the issues of isolation, marginalization, and language become bound together in his portrayals of idiots, madmen, and other prisoners. Through these characters and their idiolects, Dickens explores the politics of language—the ways in which language becomes a tool of power, and the ways in which power is created through language.

The official nineteenth-century jargon used to discuss the physically and mentally imprisoned emphasizes their shared experiences of marginalization and isolation: doctors of the insane were referred to as "alienists," and the "separate" and "silent" systems were in vogue in prison reform. The term "asylum" itself suggests a physical and legal barrier from the rest of the world, for although an asylum offers refuge and sanctuary, its "protection" is brought about by a complete severance from society—from its hazards as well as its benefits.

Throughout his representations of imprisoned characters, Dickens questions and sometimes indicts the system and the authorities that lead to the institutionalized segregation of these types, taking a perspective comparable to that of Michel Foucault in *Madness and Civilization* and *Discipline and Punish*.[3] In *Madness and Civilization*, Foucault examines the increasing confinement and the increasing linguistic segregation of the mad in modern times:

> In the serene world of mental illness, modern man no longer communicates with the madman. . . . As for a common language, there is no such thing; or rather,

there is no such thing any longer; the constitution of madness as a mental illness, at the end of the eighteenth century, affords the evidence of a broken dialogue, posits the separation as already effected, and thrusts into oblivion all those stammered imperfect words without fixed syntax in which the exchange between madness and reason was made. The language of psychiatry, which is a monologue of reason about madness, has been established only on the basis of such a silence.[4]

According to Foucault, when late-eighteenth-century insane asylum reforms ushered in more "humane" treatment, treating madness became a process of conditioning normalization; as soon as patients could consistently mimic normalized behavior, they were considered cured. Under this practice, "madness no longer exists except as seen."[5] Foucault traces another insidious and systematic process of normalization occurring in the modern and "humanized" penal system. Judges no longer simply determine whether or not a crime was committed by a certain person; now they attempt to determine *why* the crime was committed and what conditions—environmental, social, psychological—led the criminal to commit the crime. In other words, they judge the "soul" of the criminal, "and the sentence that condemns or acquits is not simply a judgement of guilt . . . it bears within it an assessment of normality and a technical prescription for a possible normalization."[6]

Dickens reveals a similar distrust of segregation, normalization, and prevailing definitions of insanity. Like Foucault, he traces the spread of disciplinary mechanisms in society, at times attacking their normalizing tendencies. Dickens rebels against a utilitarian approach to behavior, advocating a freer, unjudged, prerational psyche. Through his sympathetic idiots, madmen, and other prisoners, Dickens calls into question accepted concepts of insanity and normality. His fictional explorations of these issues prefigure Foucault's more extensive analysis over a century later. Indeed, as shall be shown below, the experiences of some Dickensian idiots and prisoners recapitulate the history of the treatment of the insane and prisoners as interpreted by Foucault.

Dickens's questioning of norms naturally leads him to a questioning of authority. What often seems most admirable about his idiots is their admission that they "know nothink," yet as an author-authority Dickens must assume a position of knowing something (BH 220; ch. 16). He partly escapes the paradox of his position by undercutting the value of sophisticated linguistic constructions in celebrating inarticulate characters, in making those trapped in private worlds and private languages the unspoken or nonsensical centers of his novels.[7] But Dickens's treatment of characters trapped in private worlds and private languages is not always so liberal or so open. He actually participates in their segregation by ultimately marginalizing them structurally in some novels of the first half of his career. The dynamic between his desire to incorporate the aberrant and an underlying urge to silence or seclude them dramatically shapes his narratives. When he is not critiquing the "discipline-mechanism[s]" that imprison and normalize, he is re-creating them in his characterizations, narrative voices, and structures.[8] These contradictory impulses lead to an odd and disturbing tension in his novels, but he seems to overcome his more conservative, restraining nature in later works. The novels I focus on in the last four chapters of this work—*Nicholas Nickleby, Barnaby Rudge, Dombey and Son,* and *Little Dorrit*—works representative of his early, middle, and late career, demonstrate an increasing liberalization and complexity in his portrayals of figures trapped in private worlds and private languages.

Throughout his career, however, Dickens failed to see, as Foucault often failed to see, that the imprisonment and isolation of *female* idiots and prisoners is exacerbated.[9] Theirs is an intensified entrapment that the author never fully acknowledges. Even in later novels, when Dickens allows his idiots and fools freer rein, when he seems to celebrate the foolish more wholeheartedly, he disciplines his women, continuing to restrain them to the norms he rebels against with other characters. Dickens's inability to recognize the intensified entrapment of women and his *participation* in their entrapment through his characterizations and narrative structures underscore his own imprisonment in a patriarchal self created through Victorian norms.[10]

Dickens's attitude toward the imprisoned changed between his fiction and nonfiction. In his nonfictional accounts of idiots, Dickens often seems to praise the institutions that have segregated them, only occasionally suggesting that segregation may not be the only answer. Moreover, as Philip Collins has shown in analyzing Dickens's magazine articles and letters, Dickens's attitude toward prisons and prisoners became increasingly conservative as he grew older.[11] It seems as if the opinions Dickens expressed in his nonfiction were always more conservative than those he expressed in his fiction, and as he got older the differences between the opinions he expressed in each grew more profound: his fictional portrayals of idiots, madmen, and prisoners became more liberal, and his nonfictional accounts, at least of prisoners, became more conservative. Reasons for these differences and changes will be examined in Chapter 2. There I also discuss Dickens's biographical connection with idiots, madmen, and other prisoners and his portrayal of them and their respective institutions in his nonfictional writings, in addition to placing his observations in perspective with his contemporaries' opinions.

Throughout his characterizations of prisoners of private worlds and languages, Dickens alludes to the holy idiots and wise fools of history, folklore, and literature through certain details of language, dress, action, and mannerism. His allusions recall similar characters who *had* a place in society, who played a role and were part of a community, characters who were valued for their abnormalities. By alluding to these historical and literary fools, Dickens implicitly asks if there is any way his society can find a place for these types and a place for their visions and language. Through them, he advocates keeping fancy and foolishness alive in a utilitarian world. In Foucault's terms, Dickens encourages the renewal of reason's dialogue with madness. He suggests that putting idiots away is not only detrimental to them but detrimental to the rest of society as well, for the roles they have played historically have been important, even vital, to the societies in which they lived. Dickens symbolically uses physical details of dress and mannerisms from the holy idiot tradition to develop a philosophy of the fool. Clothing images often link Dickens's holy fool characters particularly to Carlyle's philosophy of clothes in *Sartor Resartus*. In Chapter 3, I discuss the semiotics of the physical images that Dickens transforms from the tradition, showing how these images form major structural and thematic motifs in the novels.

Other critics have, of course, looked at isolated, abnormal types in Dickens. Leonard Manheim surveys abnormal characters in "Dickens' Fools and Madmen"; Susan Shatto's two-part article, "Miss Havisham and Mr. Mopes the Hermit: Dickens and the Mentally Ill," analyzes the treatment of two mentally aberrant characters in particular; J. Hillis Miller in *Charles Dickens: The World of His Novels* explores the general isolated plight of all of Dickens's characters but does not focus on those particularly entrapped; Michael Hollington examines Dickens's grotesques, but traces different influences on this element of Dickens's fiction and different rhetorical roles that they play; Robert Golding in *Idiolects in Dickens* does a fine job of categorizing and describing Dickens's idiolects, but he does not deal with the larger thematic and critical issues they entail; and the theme of prisons and Dickens's social commentary on them has been discussed by many renowned critics, such as Trilling and Collins, to name two of the most eminent.[12] But as yet no one has written a full-length study exploring the thematic, linguistic, structural, and imagistic interconnections of Dickens's idiots, madmen, and other prisoners and the ways Dickens uses them to comment on specific social practices, larger philosophical issues, and his own role as an author. Nor have the allusions that Dickens makes through many of these characters—particularly his idiots and madmen—been thoroughly analyzed. I do not attempt to illuminate all these allusions here, just those that play pivotal roles in the novels or have not been previously analyzed. The Foucauldian aspects of Dickens's presentation of these figures have also not been sufficiently explored, nor has anyone yet analyzed the *progress* of Dickens's treatment of idiots, madmen, and other prisoners throughout his career. Such is the territory I hope to cover in this study.

Studying this territory entails analyzing particular social issues as well as universal conditions that are described in Dickens's writings. Sometimes in Dickens's densely metaphoric portrayals of these characters, their entrapment in private languages becomes our own; their victimization by authorities and institutions becomes representative of a universal condition; their alternative realities call into question our stable, commonplace notion of reality. The idiots' idiolects merely emphasize the universal limitations of language. The madmen's visions are only a slightly intensified version of our own waking and sleeping nightmares—our own frightening sense of the slipperiness of "reality." The prisoner's scream when first confronting the confines of his narrow cell simply focuses the inescapable human anguish of confronting one prison after another from cradle to grave in a body that is itself a prison. The particular situation of each imprisoned type becomes universal because Dickens manages to create characters who are at once unique, isolated individuals and at the same time indicative of the epistemological and ontological plight of humankind.

Analyzing these imprisoned figures, then, illuminates major aspects of Dickens's imaginative vision and his understanding of society. In addition, his repeated portrayals of characters without a voice suggest that their plight is fundamental to his view of his role as an author. Dickens adopts the role of an author-authority to take up the cause of those traditionally denied authority, even authority over themselves. But his approach to the imprisoned resists simple generalizations; it changes dramatically in the course of his fiction. From the early pity with which he treats these types, he progresses to a far more complex and celebratory approach, valuing them in a way that defies all utilitarian standards. Throughout these changes, his determination to give voice to the voiceless fundamentally shapes his life and work.

NOTES

1. Some of the characters whom I discuss as "idiots" in this study may not seem at first to deserve that label, for I have included the profoundly uneducated and the illiterate because Dickens portrays them in a similar

fashion to the more typical idiots. Those characters ignorant of the workings of the world around them are as isolated as idiots, no matter what their mental capacities may be. Similarly, some of the madmen I discuss are not necessarily "mad" throughout their respective novels, but they at least exhibit or experience a spell of insanity.

2. In "Dickens and the Language of Alienation" (*English Language Notes* 16 [1978]: 117-28), Charles Schuster examines the connection between language and isolation, emphasizing that "community" and "communication" come from the same Latin root, which suggests the necessity of effective communication in maintaining ties to the community. "Dickens reveals an intuitive grasp of the relationship between communication, community, and alienation," Schuster asserts; "he does so by including in his fiction a steady outpouring of alienated individuals who demonstrate their pariah-like status by being wholly or partially inarticulate" (117).

3. See Jeremy Tambling's useful analysis of representations of prisons in Foucault and Dickens in "Prison-bound: Dickens and Foucault," *Essays in Criticism* 36, no. 1 (1986): 11-31.

4. Michel Foucault, *Madness and Civilization, A History of Insanity in the Age of Reason*, trans. Richard Howard (New York: Pantheon, 1965), x.

5. Ibid., 250.

6. Michel Foucault, *Discipline and Punish: The Birth of the Prison*, trans. Alan Sheridan (New York: Pantheon, 1977), 19-20.

7. The multiplicity of Dickens's narrative voice also indicates his ambivalence to his role as authority by avoiding a single, controlled perspective and tone. For an excellent analysis of this multiplicity, see Janet Larson, "Designed to Tell: The Shape of Language in Dickens' 'Little Dorrit' " (Ph.D. diss., Northwestern University, 1975). In *Carlyle and Dickens*, Michael Goldberg also has a good analysis of the multiplicity of Dickens's style and compares it with that of Carlyle (Athens: Univ. of Georgia Press, 1972.)

8. Foucault, *Discipline*, 209.

9. In *Disciplining Foucault* (New York: Routledge, 1991), Jana Sawicki points out that "as focused as Foucault was on domains of power/knowledge in which many of the bodies disciplined and the subjects produced and rendered docile were female, he never spoke of 'male domination' per se; he usually spoke of power as if it subjugated everyone equally" (49). In "Foucault, Femininity, and the Modernization of Patriarchal Power," Sandra Bartky concurs: "Foucault treats the body throughout as if it were one, as if the bodily experiences of men and women did not differ and as if men and women bore the same relationship to the characteristic institutions of modern life. Where is the account of the disciplinary practices that engender the 'docile bodies' of women, bodies more docile than the bodies of men?" (*Feminism and Foucault: Reflections on Resistance*, ed. Irene Diamond and Lee Quinby [Boston: Northeastern Univ. Press, 1988], 63-64). Although in *The History of Sexuality* (trans.

Robert Hurley, New York: Pantheon, 1978) Foucault does discuss the hysterization of women's bodies, in general he pays little attention to female experience as it differs from that of males (104).

10. As D. A. Miller argues in *The Novel and the Police* (Berkeley: Univ. of California Press, 1988), novelists in general perform a disciplinary function in their art; they function as "police" in their examination and recording of their subjects and in providing order and closure in conclusions (21, 93).

11. Philip Collins in the definitive *Dickens and Crime* (London: Macmillan, 1965) thoroughly explores the discrepancies between Dickens's various statements about prison reforms. Collins's work is excellent, and I am deeply indebted to it, but I would suggest that he overemphasizes Dickens's harsher statements concerning prison reform in his eagerness to prove that the traditional concept of Dickens as a lifelong liberal was inaccurate. Collins underemphasizes the attitudes that Dickens's fictional portrayals suggest, and he credits Dickens's later statements as being more indicative of his real attitudes than his earlier statements. I do not agree; however, I realize that Collins was attempting to correct the oversight of many preceding critics who had stressed Dickens's earlier, more liberal views.

12. Leonard Manheim, "Dickens' Fools and Madmen," *Dickens Studies Annual* 2 (1972): 69-97; Susan Shatto, "Miss Havisham and Mr. Mopes the Hermit: Dickens and the Mentally Ill," Part 1, *Dickens Quarterly* 2, no. 2 (1985): 43-50; Shatto, "Miss Havisham and Mr. Mopes the Hermit: Dickens and the Mentally Ill," Part 2, *Dickens Quarterly* 2, no. 3 (1985): 79-84; J. Hillis Miller, *Charles Dickens: The World of His Novels* (Cambridge, MA: Harvard Univ. Press, 1965); Michael Hollington, *Dickens and the Grotesque* (London: Croom Helm, 1984); Robert Golding, *Idiolects in Dickens: Major Techniques and Chronological Development* (London: Macmillan, 1985); Lionel Trilling, "Little Dorrit," *Dickens: A Collection of Essays*, ed. Martin Price (Englewood Cliffs, NJ: Prentice-Hall, 1967), 147-57; Philip Collins, *Dickens and Crime*, 2nd ed. (London: Macmillan, 1965).

Chapter 2

Biographical and Historical Context

Dickens's interest in various types of prisoners was sparked when his father was imprisoned for debt in the Marshalsea, and Dickens found himself alone, thrown into a harsh work environment to which he did not belong, and cut off from his family, his books, and his education. Dickens's father was imprisoned, but metaphorically Dickens was imprisoned as well. As he saw it, by being deprived of an education he had lost all chances of rising above poverty and the grueling position he held in the blacking factory in which he was forced to work to earn a living. But even before his father's imprisonment, the young Dickens had been removed from school and had begun to feel his isolation. John Forster describes how Dickens felt about this period of his life: "Many many times has he spoken to me of this, and how he seemed at once to fall into a solitary condition apart from all other boys of his own age, and to sink into a neglected state at home which had always been quite unaccountable to him."[1] Forster quotes Dickens as saying " 'what would I have given . . . to have been sent back to any other school, to have been taught something anywhere!' "[2] Clearly, what struck Dickens as being most terrible in his situation was his entrapment in solitude and ignorance. He felt condemned to the idiocy of the uneducated and the isolation of the solitary prisoner.

In an autobiographical fragment addressed to Forster, Dickens described his feelings at the time he began work in the blacking factory; although this account has often been quoted and discussed, it bears being repeated because the language Dickens used to describe this period of his life emphasizes the isolation he felt, his abhorrence of his own ignorance, and his own inarticulateness in trying to put the experience into words. Significantly, these are some of the same feelings and characteristics that he also emphasizes in his portrayals of idiots, madmen, and other prisoners:

"No words can express the secret agony of my soul . . . as I sunk into this companionship, compared these every day associates with those of my happier childhood, and felt my early hopes of growing up to be a learned and distinguished man, crushed in my breast. The deep remembrance of the sense I had of being *utterly neglected* and hopeless; of the shame I felt in my position; of *the misery it was to my young heart to believe that, day by day, what I had learned, and thought, and delighted in, and raised my fancy and my emulation up by, was passing away from me, never to be brought back any more, cannot be written.* My whole nature was so penetrated with the grief and humiliation of such considerations, that even now, famous and caressed and happy, I often forget in my dreams that I have a dear wife and children; even that I am a man; and wander desolately back to that time of my life."[3]

Just as the young Dickens was trapped in the isolation and misery of poverty, so was his experience entrapped in him. His father's imprisonment and his own employment in the blacking factory were subjects about which he remained mute for the rest of his life, with the one exception of the short autobiography he entrusted to Forster.[4] Again, the language he uses in the following passage to describe his silence emphasizes his feelings of isolation, but it also underscores his connection of psychological isolation with muteness, deafness, and blindness:

"From that hour until this at which I write, *no word of that part of my childhood which I have now gladly brought to a close, has passed my lips* to any human being. I have no idea how long it lasted; whether for a year, or much more, or less. From that hour, until this, *my father and mother have been stricken dumb upon it. I have never heard the least allusion to it,* however far off and remote, from either of them. *I have never, until I now impart it to this paper, in any burst of confidence with any one, my own wife not excepted, raised the curtain I then dropped,* thank God."[5]

Dickens's early childhood experiences of isolation and imprisonment, then, became bound together in his mind with the ideas of ignorance ("what I had learned . . . was passing away"), inarticulateness ("no words can express," "cannot be written"), muteness ("no word . . . has passed my lips," "stricken dumb"), deafness ("I have never heard"), and blindness ("the curtain . . . then dropped"). It is little wonder, therefore, that these traits are intertwined in his characterizations of imprisoned types. Unable to voice his own experiences with poverty, alienation, and marginalization, Dickens voiced, throughout his career, the experiences of others who have suffered similar plights. He recalled his childhood emotions when he later invested himself in the characterizations of his prisoners, madmen, idiots, and other entrapped, isolated characters.

ASYLUM AND PRISON REFORM

Dickens's personal interest in idiots, madmen, and other prisoners was undoubtedly fed by the debates of his contemporaries concerning reforms in the management of prisons and insane asylums throughout England. Extensive prison and asylum reforms began being implemented at the end of the eighteenth century and were much discussed throughout the nineteenth century; Dickens was certainly not the only writer to turn to them in popular magazine articles. In Dickens's own magazines, Harriet Martineau and Richard Oliver frequently contributed articles on the treatment of the insane, idiots, and deaf-mutes; W. H. Wills, coeditor of *Household Words*, contributed many articles on prisons, as did Dickens himself and other authors. The dynamic changes occurring in the number and management of these institutions raised compelling questions about the place of deviants in society and the ability (or desirability) of normalizing these deviants. Dickens never ceased addressing the issues of prison and asylum reform, and his opinions on these issues shifted radically over the course of his lifetime.

Changes in the Treatment of the Insane

The two most notable changes in the treatment of the insane during the nineteenth century were the increasing institutionalization of the insane and the gradual move away from the use of physical restraint, and what had amounted to physical abuse, toward the use of "moral" (or psychological) treatments as defined by Pinel, director of the Bicêtre, and William Tuke, director of the Quaker's York Retreat for the insane, founded in 1792. This "revolution" in psychiatric practice began during the end of the eighteenth century and continued to progress throughout the first half of the nineteenth century.

The typical eighteenth-century treatment of the insane was notoriously barbaric and cruel. The poor have always been subject to more inhumane treatment than the wealthier insane, even after the supposed "revolution" in asylum care, but in the eighteenth century even aristocrats were subject to treatment that seems in our modern eyes abhorrent and unbelievable. The Countess of Harcourt's description of the "treatment" King George III underwent for insanity makes this point vividly: " 'The unhappy patient... was no longer treated as a human being. His body was immediately encased in a machine which left no liberty of motion. He was sometimes chained to a stake. He was frequently beaten and starved, and at best he was kept in subjection by menacing and violent language.' "[6] Fear was the tool by which the patient was to be coerced into proper behavior, and whippings, beatings, " 'vomits, purges . . . surprize baths, copious bleedings and meagre diets' " were merely instruments through which fear could be produced.[7] It is little wonder that Pinel's and Tuke's moral treatment, which resisted the use of physical restraint and punishments, was considered such a welcome and humane change.

One of the prevailing eighteenth-century opinions concerning insanity had been that it was caused by disease; its origins, in other words, were considered to be primarily physical. Therefore, treating insanity via the kinds of physical "remedies" just listed was thought to be natural. Pinel and Tuke, however, believed in the psychological causes of insanity and believed, therefore, that insanity must be treated through psychological means.[8] The two resisted using physical restraints except when absolutely necessary to prevent patients from injuring themselves. The treatment they espoused was aimed at teaching the insane to exert their own inner restraints. Their method

> was designed to encourage the individual's own efforts to reassert his powers of self-control. For instead of merely resting content with the outward control of those who were no longer quite human (which had been the dominant concern of traditional responses to the mad), moral treatment actively sought to *transform* the lunatic, to remodel him into something approximating the bourgeois ideal of the rational individual.[9]

Pinel and Tuke demonstrated that their moral treatment could be used with great success. The insane could be treated in a healthy, nonhostile environment, with physical coercion used only rarely. In addition, a large number of their patients were actually "cured," meaning they never had to be readmitted to an asylum.[10]

Certainly at first glance this moral or psychological treatment seems infinitely more humane and successful than the eighteenth-century physical treatment. But there were problems with the new system as well. First of all, other asylums found it difficult to repeat the successes of Pinel and Tuke, and many areas of England (not to mention Europe and the United States) were slow in catching on to the reforms. Second, even if the successes could be repeated, the ethics of enforcing the internalization of restraint and what might seem to be a very limiting bourgeois norm have been seriously called into question by Michel Foucault and others. For Foucault, and, I will argue, for Dickens (at least part of the time), the systematized forging of *internal* chains—"that gigantic moral imprisonment which we are in the habit of calling . . . the liberation of the insane by Pinel and Tuke"—is far more frightening and certainly far more insidious than the physical abuses of the eighteenth-century treatment of the insane.[11]

Putting aside, for the moment, the philosophical objections to moral treatment, the new system faced many practical obstacles as well. Moral treatment began being instituted in asylums that were designed mostly for wealthy patients, yet the humane impulses behind the reformed approach to the insane suggested that it should also be used in pauper asylums.[12] But the spread of the reform movement to pauper asylums took a long time because county asylums were expensive to build, and justices "were slow to take up the option to pursue such an expensive innovation."[13]

In the late 1830s and 1840s the moral treatment gained some ground even in the treatment of the poor, especially when John Connolly demonstrated that paupers could be controlled without physical restraint, even in the largest pauper asylum, Hanwell, in Middlesex.[14] But Hanwell was not as successful as was first hoped. The county asylums in general did not meet with great success in using moral treatment chiefly because the number of patients in them increased too rapidly while the staffing did not. Suitable attendants were difficult to find, and with no systematic training available, the quality of care they were able to give varied widely. Also superintendents became more involved in paperwork and increasingly removed from the patients. The kind of close attention that Pinel and Tuke were able to give was no longer possible because of the increase in the size of the institutions, the number of the patients, and the related increase in bureaucratic red tape. In the "Report from the Select Committee on Lunatics" in 1859, John Connolly testified that a murder had just occurred in the Hanwell asylum due to insufficient staffing.[15] In addition, chronic cases from workhouses flooded into the county asylums. Having gone untreated for years, many of these cases were much harder to "cure" than newer cases of insanity, which usually had a high cure rate; therefore, the record of "successes" began to slip.

Construction difficulties presented another stumbling block. In order to accommodate the increasing numbers of patients, additions to asylum buildings often were constructed in a haphazard fashion, and the original buildings were not maintained properly.[16] One of the more dramatic results of haphazard construction was an increased mortality rate among patients. When the Commissioners in Lunacy investigated Haydock Lodge Lunatic Asylum in 1845-46, they determined that the high mortality rate there was caused by the constant construction of additions. Sick patients were placed in the same room as healthy ones during reconstruction, and certain areas of the building were open to the weather while other sections were deprived of any ventilation whatsoever.[17] As Walton comments, "all this made treatment and even control more difficult, and ensured a drift toward impersonality, regimentation, and the institutionalization of routine which seriously undermined pretensions to 'moral treatment.' "[18] In addition, the 1859 "Report from the Select Committee on Lunatics" revealed that there were still five or six counties in which no provisions were made at all for the insane.[19] Lunatics in these counties were often kept for life in workhouses.

Dickens was well aware of the reforms in the care of the insane that moral treatment brought about, and he was also aware that many injustices in their treatment still existed. In "The Treatment of the Insane," a two-part article in Dickens's *Household Words*, Richard Oliver examined some of the short-comings of the new asylum reforms, shortcomings that almost invariably affected the pauper asylums exclusively.[20] Inadequate provisions were made for the insane poor, Oliver claims: as of 1850, "4,699 insane patients were [still] lodged in workhouses," a situation more likely to promote than remedy their ailments.[21] Sometimes parishes would "farm out" the insane to private, unqualified individuals who took them in for profit. This practice saved the parish money but often subjected the patients to neglect and abuse. Oliver details one case in particular of an insane woman who had been farmed out to a man who kept her lying on a straw sack with her hands in handcuffs and her legs bound in an iron attached to a bed post. Oliver quotes from a letter written by the insane woman's sister to the superintendent of a local county lunatic asylum. The woman begs that her sister be readmitted to the asylum so that she can be protected from such inhumane treatment. The superinten-dent, however, was powerless to help; the responsibility lay with the parish. "It is quite clear," Oliver asserts, "that some more efficient arrangements are required for the protection of the insane poor from this grinding parochial parsimony."[22]

The kind of treatment the pauper woman received was not uncommon. The Parliamentary Papers contain numerous Select Committee Reports on the treatment of lunatics that describe patients chained naked in beds of straw sometimes for days at a time. In the 1827 "Report from the Select Committees on Pauper Lunatics in the County of Middlesex," John Nettle, who had been a patient at a private asylum called the "White House" in Bethnal Green, testified that every day he was put to bed at 3:00 in the afternoon with his hands cuffed and his leg in an iron. He would be allowed to get up at 9:00 the next morning. On weekends he was put to bed from 3:00 Saturday afternoon until Monday morning at 9:00; the whole time he was left naked in the straw, in irons, with one blanket, lying in his own filth.[23] But this practice was not limited to private asylums; even if the woman described in the "The Treatment of the Insane" had been admitted to the county asylum, she may not have fared much better. The 1852-53 "Report of the Commissioners of Lunacy on the State and Management of Bethlehem Hospital" revealed that "refractory" patients were placed naked in beds of loose straw, sometimes with a blanket, sometimes without.[24] The patients complained of "excessive cold" and of the "coarse, violent, and abusive conduct of the nurses."[25] The commissioners felt that most of the problems were caused by an insufficient number of attendants and few inspections, none at night.

Dickens was aware of these barbaric practices years before he began his career as a novelist. In a speech in 1865, he recalled being a young newspaper man and hearing newsboys describing the cruel treatment of the insane.[26] He most likely would have been aware of some of the Parliamentary Papers cited earlier, as six volumes of parliamentary reports appear in an 1844 inventory of his library,[27] and he worked as a parliamentary reporter in the early 1830s. In spite of his awareness of the treatment of the insane, however, Dickens did not seem sensitive to the particular plight of the female insane. In "A Curious Dance Around a Curious Tree," an 1852 *Household Words* article about a visit to St. Luke's Hospital for the Insane, Dickens writes that "the experience of this asylum did not differ . . . from that of similar establishments, in proving that insanity is more prevalent among women than among men."[28] Dickens does not question why more women were institutionalized for insanity; he assumes, it would seem, that women by nature were simply more disposed to mental breakdowns. He seems unaware that women were labeled insane more often than men because the range of behavior considered acceptable for females was extremely limited. As Showalter indicates in "Victorian Women and Insanity," women who were "disobedient, rebellious, or in open protest against the female role" and those who exhibited "unconventional sexual behavior" were pronounced insane and incarcerated.[29] Similar rebelliousness or promiscuity in a male would not yield the same result. Some doctors realized that the limitations of a Victorian woman's life could lead to madness, but this did not change general expectations of women or the treatment of female mental patients.[30] Showalter concludes that "mental breakdown was often an expression of resolution of conflicts in the claustrophobic middle-class feminine role, and that Victorian psychiatric labeling and incarceration was an efficient agency of sociosexual control."[31]

Apparently Dickens found little wrong with the role prescribed for women and women's increased chances of incarceration. But he did express ambivalent feelings about the institutionalization of the insane in general, as can be seen by his comment in the essay "Idiots," from *Household Words*: "... it were worth while to enquire . . . how much of the putting away of these unfortunates in past years, and how much of the putting away of many kinds of unfortunates at any time, may be attributable to that same refinement which cannot endure to be told about them."[32] Dickens suggests that the institutionalization of idiots and madmen is due to an unjustifiable and inexcusable sensitivity to what are seen as unpleasant abnormalities. He advocates, in this passage and in various fictional characterizations, a greater openness to aberrance.

Dickens's anti-institutional attitudes concerning the insane and idiots are developed most fully in his portrayals of some of his fictional characters, as will be discussed further later. John Forster shared this ambivalence toward institutionalizing idiots and the insane, and in his biography of Dickens he points out how the writer expressed his ambivalence through the characters of Betsy Trotwood and Mr. Dick in *David Copperfield*:

> By a line thrown out in *Wilhelm Meister*, that the true way of treating the insane was, in all respects possible, to act to them as if they were sane, Goethe anticipated what it took a century to apply to the most terrible disorder of humanity; and what Mrs. Trotwood does for Mr. Dick goes a step farther, by showing how often the asylums might be dispensed with, and how large might be the number of deficient intellects manageable with patience in their own homes.[33]

Dickens's negative attitudes toward institutions appear strange considering how many institutions he visited, commented upon, and helped to shape. Dickens resists institutions, but at the same time he tries to insure that they are run in the most humane and effective way possible, realizing, of course, that they are an inescapable and indispensable by-product of society. Dickens's attitudes toward institutions are never as radical as those of Foucault, but at times the two have much in common. Like Foucault, Dickens feared the increasing dominance of imprisoning structures, of "discipline-mechanism[s]," in society; the increase of asylums for the insane is just one instance.[34] There are many other ways in which society imprisons its members, and Dickens, like Foucault, explores both the literal and the figurative imprisonments, as well as the physical and mental entrapments brought about by natural defects.

Interestingly, the tone that Dickens uses in describing idiots, madmen, and other prisoners in his nonfiction often differs markedly from that which he uses to describe these types in his fiction. In his fictional accounts of idiots and madmen, as we shall see, Dickens's view tends to be more romantic, more hopeful, even more spiritual—in general, more generous, particularly in the second half of his career. But in his magazine articles describing these types, Dickens is much more the pragmatist. He is concerned with the details of the management of the institutions he visits; his accounts of the imprisoned rarely take on the kind of encompassing and metaphoric suggestiveness we shall see in his fictional descriptions. There are exceptions, of course, but for the most part Dickens's approach to idiots, madmen, and other prisoners in his magazine articles lacks romantic overtones and takes into full account the general unfavorable reactions these unfortunates produce. Dickens is well aware that these people, although fellow human beings, can be unattractive, even repulsive. For instance, in "A Curious Dance Round a Curious Tree," Dickens's description of one idiot in particular is stripped of any romantic overtones whatsoever:

> And when the sorrowful procession was closed by "Tommy," the favorite of the house, the harmless old man, with a giggle and a chuckle and a nod for every one, I think I would have rather that Tommy had charged at the tree like a Bull, than that Tommy had been at once so childish and so dreadfully un-childlike. (388)

"Tommy" would no doubt be an endearing old innocent if he had made his appearance in Dickens's fiction instead of his nonfiction. Any reader accustomed first to Dickens's fictional idiots must find the portrait here surprisingly harsh and negative.

A similar harsh tone prevails in another passage in "Idiots," in which Dickens describes a village idiot he remembers from his childhood:[35]

> As a remembrance of our own childhood in an English country town, he is a shambling knock-kneed man who was never a child, with an eager utterance of discordant sounds which he seemed to keep in his protruding forehead, a tongue too large for his mouth, and a dreadful pair of hands that wanted to ramble over everything—our own face included. But in all these cases the main idea of an idiot would be of a hopeless, irreclaimable, unimprovable being. And if he be further recalled as under restraint in a workhouse or lunatic asylum, he will still come upon the imagination as wallowing in the lowest depths of degradation and neglect: a miserable monster, whom nobody may put to death, but whom every one must wish dead, and be distressed to see alive. (313)

In his fictional portrayals of idiots, Dickens's imagery suggests a more positive perspective on those entrapped in private worlds. It is not that Dickens deals with these characters realistically in his nonfiction and non-realistically in his fiction; it is more that his concept of what constitutes "reality" seems to be broader in his fictional writings. It seems as if the engagement of the imagination and the language of the imagination encourages a more generous perspective on idiots, madmen, and prisoners and allows a vital connection between them and the rest of society to be seen. Their grotesque features are portrayed with humor; their deformities often suggest assets. They are not necessarily separate, nor do they necessarily need to be segregated. Dickens makes this point in his nonfiction as well as in his fiction, but the compelling lives and languages of his fictional idiots, madmen, and prisoners make the point more strongly than the overt admonishments resorted to more frequently in his nonfiction.

Prison Reform

A revolution was occurring at this time in prison reform as well as in the treatment of the insane. The larger movement of this revolution involved a change from a merely punitive prison system to one with the potential to reform prisoners. Like the reforms going on in the treatment of the insane, the prison reforms had an essentially moral purpose, and like the asylum reforms, they began being instituted toward the end of the eighteenth century. The prison reform movement eventually suffered much the same fate as the asylum reform movement; by the end of the nineteenth century, all the new methods that had been greeted with so much hope were being abandoned. Under the superintendence of Sir Edmund DuCane, who was appointed Assistant Director of Convict Prisons in 1863, the idea of trying to reform prisoners was dropped in favor of increasing the punitive and deterring potential of the convict prisons.[36]

Within this larger movement from merely punitive, to reformatory, back to merely punitive prisons, a smaller battle occurred between the "separate" and "silent" systems of prison management. Sir Joshua Jebb promoted the separate system and designed a model prison based on this school of thought. The model "separate" prison isolated each prisoner in a single cell where he was kept in solitary confinement. "Reform," according to Philip Priestley, "was to be brought about by the influences of solitude, prayer, simple work, and the ministrations of sober, upright and god-fearing attendants."[37] Priestley describes this system as "an expensive failure" because the buildings were costly to construct and the system drove many prisoners insane. The "silent" system operated under a similar principle but allowed the prisoners to be together, albeit silent, during work and worship.

One of the impetuses behind separate and silent prisons was a desire to prevent the corruption that occurred, particularly in urban prisons, when criminals were allowed to associate with each other and with the innocent, who, before their trials, were thrown in the same cells as the convicted. In 1835 the "First and Second Reports from the Select Committee of the House of Lords Appointed to Inquire into the Present State of the Several Gaols and Houses of Correction in England and Wales" argued that "imprisonment in Newgate, Giltspur Street, and the Borough Compter . . . must have the effect of corrupting the . . . Inmates, and manifestly tend to the Extension rather than to the Suppression of Crime."[38] One of the witnesses brought forth in this report was Matthew Newman, principal turnkey of Newgate. He was asked, "Since you have been at Newgate have you ever heard it asserted, that Crimes of a disgusting Nature have been attempted in Newgate?" His answer was "I have. . . . I understood there was a Man who had Connexion with another, and he had attempted it with another also. . . ."[39] The same committee concludes, in highly suggestive language, that

> the greatest Mischief is proved . . . to follow from the Intercourse which is still permitted in many Prisons: the comparatively innocent are seduced, the unwary are entrapped, and the Tendency to Crime in Offenders not entirely hardened is confirmed by the Language, the Suggestions, and the Example of more depraved and systematic Criminals.[40]

The double-entendres of the passage suggest that the fear of sexual "Connexion" among prisoners was one of the main motivations behind isolation.

Through his experience as a parliamentary reporter and his visits to prisons, Dickens no doubt became aware of the reports of sodomy and the advantages of the separate system in preventing it. Nevertheless, during the 1840s, he clearly abhorred the separate and silent systems and openly attacked them in his comments on prisons in the United States and elsewhere. His reaction shows little awareness of some of the motivations behind the new systems, but instead demonstrates a purely humanitarian concern for the harshness of the punishment. In *American Notes* Dickens criticizes Philadelphia's Eastern Penitentiary, which was run on the separate system:

> . . . I am persuaded that those who devised this system of Prison Discipline, and those benevolent gentlemen who carry it into execution, do not know what it is that they are doing. I believe that very few men are capable of estimating the immense amount of torture and agony which this dreadful punishment, pro-

longed for years, inflicts upon the sufferers; and in guessing at it myself, and in reasoning from what I have seen written upon their faces, and what to my certain knowledge they feel within, I am only the more convinced that there is a depth of terrible endurance in it which none but the sufferers themselves can fathom, and which no man has a right to inflict upon his fellow-creature. (99)

He further describes the system of Philadelphia's Eastern Penitentiary as "rigid, strict, and . . . in its effects . . . cruel and wrong" (*AN* 99). To him, long years of solitary confinement were the cruelest and most agonizing means of torture, capable of dementing the human psyche:

I hold this slow and daily tampering with the mysteries of the brain, to be immeasurably worse than any torture of the body: and because its wounds are not upon the surface, and it extorts few cries that human ears can hear: therefore I the more denounce it, as a secret punishment which slumbering humanity is not roused up to stay. (*AN* 99)

The final comment about "slumbering humanity" not being "roused up" yet suggests a connection between isolation or marginalization and rebellion, a connection that Dickens will continue to make, and make more strongly, in his fiction. Isolation yielding revolt is an equation Dickens works out throughout his writings. Clearly he had a deeply held belief that being cut off from communication with others was one of the most agonizing fates, and to deliberately isolate a fellow human being was the ultimate injustice. Since Dickens believed that the ability to communicate is what makes us human (as we shall see explicitly later in his description of a deaf, dumb, and blind girl's subhuman state before she learned sign language), then prohibiting communication is prohibiting prisoners from being human; in other words, it is enforcing their degradation to a bestial state.

But Dickens was horrified by solitary confinement (both literal and metaphorical) for other reasons as well. He imagined that, trapped within oneself, one would eventually be haunted by spirits. Ghosts become a recurrent image in Dickens's portrayals of individuals trapped in extreme privacy. In "Nurse's Stories," one of the essays in *The Uncommercial Traveller*, Dickens questions the lack of ghosts in Robinson Crusoe's account of his isolation: "So is the site of the hut where Robinson lived with the dog and the parrot and the cat, and where he endured those first agonies of solitude, which—strange to say—never involved any ghostly fancies; a circumstance so very remarkable, that perhaps he left out something in writing his record?" (149) In a letter to Forster (April 3, 1842) Dickens reveals similar thoughts upon visiting a solitary prison in Pittsburgh:

"At Pittsburgh I saw another solitary confinement prison. . . . A horrible thought occurred to me when I was recalling all I had seen, that night. *What if ghosts be one of the terrors of the jails?* I have pondered on it often since then. The utter solitude by day and night; the many hours of darkness; the silence of death; the mind for ever brooding on melancholy themes, and having no relief . . . imagine a prisoner covering up his head in the bedclothes and looking out from time to time, with a ghastly dread of some inexplicable silent figure that always sits upon his bed, or stands . . . in the same corner of his cell. The more I think of it, the more certain I feel that not a few of these men . . . are nightly visited by spectres."[41]

In his fiction, Dickens's criminals often experience similar ghostly visions; his madmen and idiots are frequently susceptible to visions as well, but usually they are more positive, the visions of some of the idiots being almost divine at times. Dickens portrays these isolated characters as being closer to or more aware of an alternate reality the more they are cut off from the everyday reality of normalized characters. The nature of sanity and even reality itself is called into question through the visions of those in solitude. The specter just described could indicate that the confinement of the solitary prisoner has warped his mind; on another level, however, the specter could be a manifestation of the prisoner's conscience, or a presence to which anyone but a solitary prisoner would be too desensitized. In this portrayal and others like it, Dickens seems to be presenting, as Carlyle did, the possibility of a spiritual level of existence coexistent with and accessible to our own. The issue of Dickens's (and Carlyle's) fascination with ghosts will be discussed more fully later; for now it is enough to point out that Dickens repeatedly makes a connection between isolation and specters, just as he makes a connection between isolation and revolt, in both his nonfiction and his fiction.

Dickens clearly conveyed his unfavorable first reactions to the separate prison system, but he had negative first impressions of the silent system as well when visiting the jail at Lausanne in 1846.[42] The prison had been recently run according to the separate system, but M. Verdeil, the physician, "had observed so many cases of mental affections, terrible fits, and madness attaining to such alarming heights among them that he had formed a party that brought about its abolition."[43] Dickens was startled at the similarities in the physical and mental disturbances brought about by the system in Lausanne and in Philadelphia, and he was interested to see his first impressions confirmed by a medical authority.[44] Dickens found the silent system, with which Verdeil had replaced the separate system, almost as inhumane because of the long sentences that were given. In a letter to Forster on July 25-26, 1846, Dickens writes, "The sentences . . . are very terrible. I saw one man sent there for murder under circumstances of mitigation—for 30 years. Upon the silent social system all the time!"[45]

Dickens's criticisms of the separate and silent systems were well-founded. In spite of some of the legitimate motivations behind the institution of these systems, in practice they were often dehumanizing. The cell in which a solitary prisoner was kept for the duration of his or her stay was extremely small, usually around seven feet long, seven feet high, and four feet across. It was not unusual to hear prisoners cry out and beg for mercy upon their first sight of their new homes.[46] In addition to being cramped, the cells were dark, and few had the benefit even of the chink of light Dickens describes in many of his depictions of the cells of his fictional prisoners. Ventilation in most prisons was notoriously bad, and even the most hardened criminals found the odors nauseating. Food rations were meager and unvaried, and it was common to find worms in the gruel. Some of the more amusing aspects of prison life were the ludicrous architectural practices that were necessary to keep inmates separate. The chapel was constructed to sit each prisoner in a vertical telephone booth-like enclosure that separated him from his fellow prisoners. The enclosures are described by one prisoner as " 'upright coffins.' "[47] The treadwheel, under the separate system, had to be constructed similarly, each prisoner treading in an enclosure walled off from his fellows. In the separate system, prisoners spent most of their terms within one cramped box after another.

Although the surroundings were uncomfortable, even unhealthy at times, most prisoners found the lack of communication hardest to bear. The prisoners' desire to speak or yell was sometimes uncontrollable. Prohibited speech, the prisoners devised ingenious methods for communicating with each other. Messages were scraped on food tins, holes were bored in the walls between cells, refuse pipes in the W.C. were used for speaking tubes. A system of knocks or raps was also used to communicate between cells.[48] In "Pet Prisoners," a *Household Words* article, Dickens describes another means of communication between prisoners: "Small pieces of paper with writing upon them, [were] crushed into balls, and shot into the apertures of cell doors, by prisoners passing along the passages" (99). Sometimes a prisoner could sneak a few words in during exercise even though the guards closely watched the prisoners' lips. A more successful means was using the cover of hymns in chapel service to insert a few words to a neighboring prisoner.[49] But in spite of their ingenuity in producing these *very* private idiolects, little communication could take place. Trapped within themselves, many prisoners feared going insane. The idea behind both the separate and the silent systems was that the prisoner would be forced to turn inward, reevaluate his or her life, and repent. But the effects of solitary confinement were rarely so positive. Many prisoners did go mad. Those who managed to keep their sanity lived with the constant fear of madness.[50]

In spite of his early and just criticisms of the undue harshness of the separate and silent systems, Dickens, in "Pet Prisoners" (April 27, 1850), criticizes these same systems in England for being too lenient. In this *Household Words* article, Dickens's main objections to the separate system as instituted in England, particularly in Pentonville Penitentiary, are that it is too expensive and the convicted criminals receive better food than workhouse prisoners, who are guilty of nothing more than poverty. Dickens compares the average cost of maintaining one prisoner under the separate system with the yearly earnings of an average worker and reveals that the prisoner costs five pounds more than an average worker's yearly salary, with which he must feed, clothe, and shelter himself and his family. Dickens also objects to the radically different treatment received by prisoners who are not in one of these "model prisons." "Pet prisoners"—those in the new model prisons—lead a life of luxury compared to prisoners in older jails, even though their crimes are similar. Dickens's description of the emotional effects of solitary confinement also differs radically in this article from his sympathetic accounts of the "torture and agony" undergone by solitary prisoners in the United States (*AN* 99). In "Pet Prisoners" Dickens suggests that the real emotional and spiritual drawback to the solitary system is that it fosters egotism: "The state of mind into which a man is brought who is the lonely inhabitant of his own small world . . . we believe in most cases to have very little promise in it . . . A strange absorbing selfishness—a spiritual egotism and vanity, real or assumed—is the first result" (99). Compare this assessment of the state of solitary prisoners to his description in *American Notes* of their "depth of terrible endurance . . . which none but the sufferers themselves can fathom" (*AN* 99). The alternative that Dickens advocates is the silent system, which was less expensive to operate, but which he had also denounced earlier.

What changed Dickens's opinion so radically? There are several ways of interpreting this shift in attitude. First, the separate system used in England was not as strict as that used in America. In England the period of solitary confinement was usually less than a year and no more than a year and a half, as Dickens indicates in "Pet Prisoners" (97); therefore, the threat of insanity was not as much of a problem. But Michael Goldberg in *Carlyle and Dickens* attributes Dickens's shift in attitude to the influence of Carlyle. Both men's conservatism, according to Goldberg, developed as a reaction against their earlier, liberal/romantic ideals with which they had become increasingly frustrated. Reform was necessary, but the means to bring it about did not seem to exist. Liberal attitudes and liberal programs appeared to be ineffective. Seeing this, Carlyle turned increasingly harsh and conservative in his writings, and Dickens, whom Goldberg sees as continually trying to please his mentor, followed suit.[51] But, as Goldberg indicates, "Dickens' harsher side which derives so much of its rancor and animus from Carlyle . . . remained almost totally unrecognized by the man whom above all it was designed to please."[52]

There is another explanation for the shift in Dickens's attitude, however. Dickens often takes a more conservative, pragmatic stand in his journalism than he does in his fiction and his longer nonfictional accounts such as *American Notes*, as we have seen above in his nonfictional writings about idiots and madmen. Goldberg also makes this distinction between Dickens's fiction and nonfiction:

> Doubtless some of these discrepancies and inconsistencies in Dickens' commitments on social problems depend upon whether one is consulting Dickens' novels or his more occasional writings. As K. J. Fielding points out in his edition of Dickens' speeches, although Dickens "was deeply concerned about contemporary affairs in both his public life and his fiction, they never quite correspond."[53]

Collins makes this distinction as well.[54] An additional explanation of the discrepancy in Dickens's opinion is that he may have begun feeling that prisoners, whether or not they were in solitary confinement, were becoming less isolated and marginalized than the average impoverished workman. Having been given so much attention during the prison reform debates, prisoners no longer occupied as marginal a status, perhaps, as the working man or woman whose plight was less dramatic and overt. Dickens may have revised his opinions simply to emphasize the cause of those he felt were even more isolated and imprisoned, in their own way, than typical prisoners.

In spite of Dickens's increasingly conservative attitude toward prisoners in his nonfiction, in his fiction he continued to portray them sympathetically throughout his career; in fact his portrayals became even more sympathetic. The penultimate completed novel of his career features one of the most sympathetic criminals in all his novels—Magwitch—and Pip, the hero of the novel, is his conspirator in crime. Jeremy Tambling emphasizes Pip's criminal nature: "[Pip's] sense of criminality is fed by virtually each act and its consequences that he undertakes."[55] In fact, Goldberg states that Great Expectations suggests the inherent criminal nature of all humankind.[56] The way Dickens imaginatively invests himself in the feverish criminal exploits of Bradley Headstone in *Our Mutual Friend* and Jasper in *The Mystery of Edwin*

Drood indicates that his sympathy for and attraction to the criminal remained intact until the end of his career, even though he did not continue to empathize with them in his nonfiction.

Therefore, in spite of some of his unsympathetic responses to solitary prisoners and criminals in general, Dickens continued to portray their lives sympathetically in his fiction just as he had in his earlier career in his nonfiction, even though he certainly advocates punishment for them. Of course, he is far more sympathetic to his noncriminal imprisoned types, such as idiots and madmen. Dickens finds their isolation truly tragic. Clearly the separate and silent systems, whether or not they led to "pet prisoners," emphasized and reinforced the isolating and exclusionary nature of prisons. Prisons by definition segregate criminals from the rest of society, but prisons under the separate and silent system took that segregation one step further and isolated the prisoners from each other. The increasing institutionalization of idiots and the insane at this time also emphasized the exclusion and isolation of abnormal types. This growing tendency toward isolating undesirables from the mainstream of society is one whose pragmatic values are obvious but whose ethical implications and tendencies are questionable. Dickens does question them in his travel narratives and magazine articles, and he continues to question them in his portraits of fictional characters, at once recognizing the need to protect society from its dangerous members and to protect its members from society.

OTHER PRISONERS, OTHER PRISONS

Dickens's interest in, visits to, and writings about the imprisoned were not limited to criminals, idiots, and madmen alone. He also visited workhouses and institutes for the deaf, dumb, and blind and wrote movingly about several particular inmates of these institutions. In "A Wapping Workhouse," an essay that first appeared in *All the Year Round* and formed part of the *Uncommercial Traveller* series, Dickens describes a particularly intriguing facet of the communication barrier involving workhouse prisoners. In the essay, Dickens describes how images of his visit to a workhouse stick with him after he leaves; when he tries to push them out of his mind, the words of one prisoner in particular haunt him. This particular prisoner seems fairly resigned to his imprisonment, but he objects to his isolation being unduly emphasized by the warden. "I have a complaint to make against the master," he tells Dickens. "The master and myself are both masons, sir, and I make him the sign continually; but, because I am in this unfortunate position, sir, he won't give me the countersign." It is little wonder that these words, rich in metaphoric and political significance, reverberate for Dickens. Here we see a prisoner who makes a "sign" (signs being, of course, the basis of language) that should effect communication between himself and his "master" (another well-chosen, politically significant word), but it does not, not because the prisoner's language is too private, but because the "master" chooses not to recognize the sign—chooses not to respond to the prisoner's language—since the prisoner is an undesirable communicant. Refusing to comprehend the language of a type or class of people is an effective political tool—it marginalizes those one wishes to ignore and segregate, and it emphasizes one's own power. Moreover, like the practice of solitary confinement, it deprives the undesirable of human status by stripping him of the ability to communicate; after all, in a Heideggerian perspective, "The ability to speak is what marks man as man."[57]

Those trapped within private worlds because of their inabilities to see, hear, and speak held a particular fascination for Dickens. In *American Notes* he describes how "deeply moved" he was by his visit to the Perkins Institute for the Blind in Boston on his first trip to the United States. He was impressed with Samuel Gridley Howe's progress in teaching the blind, deaf, and dumb children to communicate. Dickens felt that until these children learned how to communicate, they were scarcely human, a notion shared by many of his contemporaries and twentieth-century linguists as well, as mentioned earlier.[58] No one could be more profoundly trapped in privacy than the deaf, dumb, and blind; yet their situation was not entirely hopeless. It was Howe's ability to shed a pale light on the rims of these children's minds that so fascinated Dickens. One deaf, dumb, and blind girl in particular caught his attention—and the attention of many other nineteenth-century visitors as well—Laura Bridgman. Dickens was moved by the way in which her human qualities were "inclosed within her delicate frame. . . . [with] but one outward sense—the sense of touch" (*AN* 32). Before she learns to understand and use sign language, these human qualities are entirely locked within her; she exists only as an animal. He describes her state in terms of a solitary prisoner: "There she was, before me; built up, as it were, in a marble cell, impervious to any ray of light, or particle of sound; with her poor white hand peeping through a chink in the wall, beckoning to some good man for help, that an Immortal soul might be awakened" (*AN* 32).[59]

That Dickens felt a deep connection among prisoners, workhouse inmates, idiots, and the deaf, dumb, and blind is emphasized by the imagery he uses (and borrows) in describing these different yet similar types. Details of clothing and features, which will be discussed more fully later, are often startlingly similar in his descriptions of the mentally and physically imprisoned. But the most striking repeated visual image is that of the "chink in the wall" used in the passage describing Laura Bridgman. Dickens repeatedly uses the phrase "chink in the wall," or the image of light pouring through a chink, to describe the one means of illumination, literal or figurative, available to the solitary prisoner, the idiot, the madman, and the deaf, dumb, and blind. The chink suggests the severe limitations of their situations, and yet, at the same time, it emphasizes that their position is not entirely hopeless. Some light is accessible to them: they can be reached.

The phrase "chink in the wall" occurs again in *American Notes* when Dickens describes a solitary prisoner in a New York jail. Dickens is horrified that the prisoners are never let out to exercise, even more horrified when he looks into one of the cramped and stuffy cells:

> A small bare cell, into which the light enters through a high *chink in the wall*. There is a rude means of washing, a table, and a bedstead. Upon the latter, sits a man of sixty; reading. He looks up for a moment; gives an impatient dogged shake; and fixes his eyes upon his book again. As we withdraw our heads, the door closes on him, and is fastened as before. (*AN* 84; emphasis added)

This prisoner, accused of murdering his wife, and rendered, for all practical purposes, mute, deaf, and blind by his imprisonment, has only the "high chink in the wall," as did Laura Bridgman, for illumination. Marcus Stone's illustration for the "Philadelphia" chapter of *American Notes* shows a solitary prisoner in his cell, sitting on his bed in a thin wedge of light let in through a narrow window—an image that captures the sense of a "chink in the wall."

Before *American Notes*, Dickens had used the chink in the wall and the shaft of light images in "A Visit to Newgate," Chapter 25 of *Sketches by Boz*, when describing a prisoner in the press room, awaiting his sentence: "His cheek rested upon his hand; and, with his face a little raised, and his eyes wildly staring before him, *he seemed to be unconsciously intent on counting the chinks in the opposite wall*" (211; emphasis added). Dickens continues to use the chink-in-the-wall image to describe the situations of some of his fictional and nonfictional characters. The Marchioness in The Old Curiosity Shop peers at the sordid world outside her dungeon through a chink in the door (426; ch. 57, 481-82; ch. 64). In *Barnaby Rudge*, Barnaby and Lord George Gordon are each pictured sitting in a wedge of light let in by a chink in the wall of his prison cell—Barnaby is pictured so twice (448; ch. 58, 568; ch. 74, 584; ch. 76). These illustrations bear a striking resemblance to Marcus Stone's illustration of a prisoner in *American Notes*, although the *Barnaby Rudge* illustrations were executed by George Cattermole and Hablot K. Browne. In "A Wapping Workhouse," Dickens describes one of the imprisoned idiot women sitting on the floor with "a gleam of the mid-day sun" shining on her (22). And Dr. Manette in *A Tale of Two Cities* is first seen working in a scant beam of light let through by a chink in the window (37-39; chs. 5-6). The image is a resonant and recurring one for Dickens. It binds together the idiot, the prisoner, the madman, and the deaf, dumb, and blind—the "guilty" as well as the "innocent." Ultimately, through its repetition and its suggestiveness, it places the seemingly unimprisoned in the same epistemological and ontological situation as the imprisoned.

Dickens continued his observation of the deaf, dumb, and blind at the Blind Institution in Lausanne in 1846, taking particular interest in two patients. One, a young boy, had been taught to speak a little—something that had been considered impossible before. The patient was fond of cigars, so Dickens regularly brought him some. Before Dickens left the area, the boy had been taught to say "M. Dickens m'a donne les cigares," a feat with which Dickens was much impressed.

Dickens was equally impressed with the work being done there with a deaf, dumb, and blind ten-year-old girl. When she was first brought in, she could not even control her bodily functions and spent much time crouching in the fetal position. The institute managed at least to make her appearance more civilized: " 'They have got her out of that strange, crouching position; dressed her neatly; and accustomed her to have a pleasure in society. She laughs frequently, and also claps her hands and jumps; having, God knows how, some inward satisfaction.' "[60] Cut off from every sense but that of touch, this young girl seems to have some inner resource or alternate reality from which she derives satisfaction. Like the prisoner, the idiot, and the madman she turns inward, but what she sees there must remain a mystery since she is unable to communicate. Some of the idiots in Dickens's fiction find a similar source of amusement, inaccessible to others. Barnaby Rudge is fascinated by the most mundane details in his environment—things unnoticed by others, such as clothes dancing on a clothesline (*BR* 81; ch. 10). The Aged P, rendered idiotic by extreme deafness and perhaps senility, takes great delight in nods (*GE* 196-97; ch. 25).

The tutors of the deaf, dumb, and blind girl in Lausanne do manage to reach her eventually through music:

"I never saw a more tremendous thing in its way, in my life, than when they stood her, t'other day, in the center of a group of blind children who sang a chorus to the piano; and brought her hand, and kept it, in contact with the instrument. A shudder pervaded her whole being, her breath quickened, her colour deepened,—and I can compare it to nothing but returning animation in a person nearly dead. It was really awful to see how the sensation of the music fluttered and stirred the locked-up soul within her."[61]

Dickens expresses much hope for both of the deaf, dumb, and blind patients in Lausanne, but he was disappointed upon returning in 1853 to find that the young boy did not remember him, nor had he made any meaningful use of the language he had learned. He would sit for hours simply repeating rhyming words. The young girl had shown no progress and had been dismissed years earlier as an idiot.[62] Obviously the solitude in which these two patients were entrapped was much more profound than either Dickens or their doctors and tutors had predicted. Making the abnormal "normal" often proved more difficult than had been hoped. As discussed earlier, the failures in asylum and prison reforms were revealing the same problem. Perhaps these failed attempts at normalization influenced Dickens's questioning of the impulse to normalization in general. Certainly, by the midpoint in his career, as we shall see, he began to restrain himself from normalizing and marginalizing his fictional eccentrics as he had done in earlier novels, allowing them a freer range of aberrant behavior.

At the beginning of this chapter, I discussed Dickens's feelings of isolation and imprisonment as a boy, and I suggested that these feelings influenced his adult interest in the isolated and imprisoned around him. But just because Dickens's focus turned outward does not mean that he overcame his personal feelings of entrapment and isolation; these feelings haunted him throughout his adult life. Through a frenzied career as author and editor, through a broken marriage, through a feverish and fatal tour of readings, Dickens never overcame his solitary confinement:

Like William Dorrit, Dickens has felt himself walled in behind the barriers of social humiliations and shames; like Dr. Manette, [Dickens] has known the solitary confinement of the man of talent, shut away within his own breast from all the deep companionship of understanding. Deeply, painfully reserved, he had never been able to express, not even to Forster, the one man who knew the facts, the full intensity of his hurt. But his very silence seemed to him the universal fate: "every beating heart," he exclaimed, "is, in some of its imaginings, a secret to the heart nearest it."[63]

With Dickens's childhood experience of poverty and imprisonment, his lifelong experience of isolation, and the climate of asylum and prison reform around him throughout his life, it is little wonder that idiots, madmen, and prisoners are featured so often in his writings. But, as has been suggested throughout this chapter, Dickens does more than comment on the practices he saw around him and describe the characters he met in his daily life; he takes these characters and through them explores complex psychological and philosophical issues, questioning all the while some fundamental assumptions upon which modern society is based.

NOTES

1. John Forster, *Life of Charles Dickens* (New York: Hearst's, n.d.), 14.
2. Ibid., 14.
3. Quoted in Edgar Johnson, *Charles Dickens: His Tragedy and Triumph*, 2 vols. (New York: Simon and Schuster, 1952), 34. Emphasis added.
4. There is some dispute about whether or not Dickens shared the autobiography with his family. Johnson asserts that Dickens's wife and children did not learn his history until after his death when they read Forster's biography (*Charles Dickens: His Tragedy and Triumph*, 2 vols. [New York: Simon and Schuster, 1952], 44). But according to Charles Dickens, Jr., Dickens did show this autobiographical fragment to Catherine, who urged him not to publish it because it " 'defamed his mother and father' " (quoted in Ackroyd, *Dickens* [New York: HarperCollins, 1990], 553). Slater speculates that Catherine might have lied about having seen the fragment in order to present a more favorable picture of her relationship with her husband, but he does not feel this is likely (*Dickens and Women* [Stanford, CA: Stanford Univ. Press, 1983], 157).
5. Quoted in Johnson, *Charles Dickens*, 44. Emphasis added.
6. Quoted in Andrew Scull, ed., *Madhouses, Mad-Doctors, and Madmen: The Social History of Psychiatry in the Victorian Era* (London: Athlone Press, 1981), 107.
7. Ibid., 108.
8. William F. Bynum, Jr., "Rationales for Therapy in British Psychiatry, 1780-1835," in *Madhouses, Mad-Doctors, and Madmen: The Social History of Psychiatry in the Victorian Era*, ed. Andrew Scull (London: Athlone Press, 1981), 42.
9. Scull, *Madhouses*, 111.
10. Ibid., 112.
11. Michel Foucault, *Madness and Civilization: A History of Insanity in the Age of Reason*, trans. Richard Howard (New York: Pantheon, 1965), 278.
12. John Walton, "The Treatment of Pauper Lunatics in Victorian England: The Case of Lancaster Asylum, 1816-1870," in *Madhouses, Mad-Doctors,*

and Madmen: The Social History of Psychiatry in the Victorian Era, ed. Andrew Scull (London: Athlone Press, 1981), 166.

13. Ibid., 167.

14. Ibid., 168.

15. "Report from the Select Committee on Lunatics" [1859], *British Parliamentary Papers*, Health: Mental, vol. 3 (Shannon: Irish Univ. Press, 1968), 165.

16. Walton, "Treatment of Pauper Lunatics," 168-70.

17. "Report of Commissioners in Lunacy Relative to the Haydock Lodge Lunatic Asylum" [1847], *British Parliamentary Papers*, Health: Mental, vol. 6 (Shannon: Irish Univ. Press, 1969), 41.

18. Walton, "Treatment of Pauper Lunatics," 169.

19. "Report from Select Committee on Lunatics," 6.

20. Richard Oliver, "The Treatment of the Insane," *Household Words* 6 Sept. 1851: 572-76; 5 June 1852: 270-73.

21. Ibid., 573.

22. Ibid., 573-74.

23. "Report from the Select Committees on Pauper Lunatics in the County of Middlesex" [1826-27], *British Parliamentary Papers*, Health: Mental, vol. 2 (Shannon: Irish Univ. Press, 1968), 37.

24. "Report of the Commissioners of Lunacy as to the State and Management of Bethlehem Hospital" [1852-53], *British Parliamentary Papers*, Health: Mental, vol. 6 (Shannon: Irish Univ. Press, 1969), 14.

25. Ibid., 20.

26. Peter Ackroyd, *Dickens* (New York: HarperCollins, 1990), 136.

27. *The Letters of Charles Dickens*, Pilgrim ed., vol. 4 (Oxford: Clarendon Press, 1977), 724.

28. Quoted in Elaine Showalter, "Victorian Women and Insanity," in *Madhouses, Mad-Doctors, and Madmen: The Social History of Psychiatry in the Victorian Era*, ed. Andrew Scull (London: Athlone Press, 1981), 313.

29. Ibid., 324.

30. Ibid., 326.

31. Ibid.

32. Charles Dickens and W. H. Wills, "Idiots," *Household Words*, 4 June 1853: 316. Harry Stone suggests that the first paragraph and the last three-and-a-half pages were written by Dickens (plus various interjections throughout). The passage I quote here comes from the last three-and-a-half pages (*Charles Dickens' Uncollected Writings from Household Words 1850-1859*, vol. 2 [Bloomington: Indiana Univ. Press, 1968], 489).

33. Forster, Life, 136.

34. Foucault, Discipline and Punish: The Birth of the Prison, trans. Alan Sheridan (New York: Pantheon, 1977), 209.

35. This passage is from the opening paragraph of "Idiots"; according to Harry Stone, this is one of the passages that Dickens contributed to the essay (*Charles Dickens' Uncollected Writings from Household Words 1850-1859*, vol. 2 [Bloomington: Indiana Univ. Press, 1968], 489).

36. Philip Priestley, *Victorian Prison Lives: English Prison Biography 1830-1914* (London: Methuen, 1985), 6.

37. Ibid.

38. "First and Second Reports from the Select Committee of the House of Lords on the Present State of the Several Gaols and Houses of Correction in England and Wales with Minutes of Evidence and Appendices" [1835], British Parliamentary Papers, Crime and Punishment, vol. 3 (Shannon: Irish Univ. Press, 1968), iii.

39. Ibid., 313-14.

40. Ibid., v.

41. Quoted in Forster, *Life*, 281.

42. There seems to be some confusion about whether the jail in Lausanne was run according to the separate or the silent system. In a letter to Forster, Dickens says it is modeled after the Philadelphia system, which is the separate system, but in the same letter he also refers to it as the "silent social system" (Philip Collins, *Dickens and Crime*, 2nd ed. [London: Macmillan, 1965], 131). Collins discusses the Lausanne jail as a model of the separate system, but Edgar Johnson refers to it as a silent system prison (*Charles Dickens: His Tragedy and Triumph*, 2 vols. [New York: Simon and Schuster, 1952], 599). In fact, the prison had been run on the separate system, but M. Verdeil, the prison physician, campaigned to have it abolished. He succeeded, and it was abolished except in cases when the imprisonment did not exceed ten months. Verdeil instituted the silent system instead, which Dickens also found inhumane due to the long sentences (*The Letters of Charles Dickens*, Pilgrim ed, vol. 4 [Oxford: Clarendon Press, 1977], 589).

43. Johnson, *Charles Dickens*, 599.

44. Ibid.

45. *The Letters of Charles Dickens*, Pilgrim ed., vol. 4 (Oxford: Clarendon Press, 1977), 589.

46. Priestley, *Victorian Prison Lives*, 29.

47. Quoted in ibid., 92.

48. Ibid., 46-47.

49. Ibid., 87, 94-95.

50. Collins, *Dickens and Crime*, 62; Priestley, *Victorian Prison Lives*, 42.

51. Michael Goldberg, *Carlyle and Dickens* (Athens: Univ. of Georgia Press, 1972), 131-55.

52. Ibid., 155.

53. Ibid., 155.

54. Collins, *Dickens and Crime*, 90; also see Robert Rothburn's dissertation, "Dickens' Periodical Essays and Their Relationships to the Novels" (Ph.D. diss., University of Minnesota, 1957). Rothburn examines how Dickens in his periodical essays advocates strict punishments for criminals and celebrates the achievements of the police, even though criminals in his fiction are often depicted heroically.

55. Jeremy Tambling, "Prison-bound: Dickens and Foucault," *Essays in Criticism* 36, no. 1 (1986): 22.

56. Goldberg, *Carlyle and Dickens*, 157.

57. Martin Heidegger, *On the Way to Language*, trans. P. D. Hertz (New York: Harper & Row, 1971), 112.

58. Wittgenstein adheres to this belief: " '[Outside of language] I cannot recognize the human in the human' " (quoted in *Wittgenstein and Phenomenology* [Albany: SUNY Press, 1981], 203).

59. In "Laura Bridgman and Little Nell," Elisabeth Gitter states that Dickens's description of Laura was taken from Howe's description in the *Ninth Annual Report to the Trustees of the Perkins Institution* (*Dickens Quarterly* 8, no. 2 [1991]: 75-79). "Even the image of living entombment with which Dickens introduces his discussion of Bridgman is borrowed from Howe, who had used it not only in the 1841 *Report* quoted by Dickens, but as early as 1838, in his first accounts of her," Gitter relates (76). Gitter goes on to indicate that Dickens found much in the description and the girl that might have reminded him of Little Nell. Even though he didn't write the description himself, his decision to use it is just as significant.

60. Quoted in Forster, *Life*, 476.

61. Quoted in ibid., 476.

62. Ibid., 167-68.

63. Johnson, *Charles Dickens*, 973.

Chapter 3

Holy Idiots / Wise Fools:
Traditions and Transformations

In portraying fictional figures trapped in private worlds and private languages, Dickens often alludes to elements of the holy idiot and wise fool traditions. He is influenced primarily by idiots and fools of history, Judeo-Christian traditions, folklore, Shakespeare, and the Romantics.[1] Of course, these sources are interrelated. Historic fools, such as village idiots and fools in Roman noblemen's households, in medieval festival plays, and in royal courts, influenced folklore fools; both informed Shakespeare's famous portrayals of fools; and all three influenced Romantic concepts of fools and idiots, for instance Wordsworth's "The Idiot Boy" and Scott's Madge Wildfire and Davie Gellatley. It is not my intention to give a history of these treatments but to examine some of the their implications and to suggest how Dickens uses and transforms certain elements, such as physical deformities, motley clothes, heightened spirituality, and the fool's challenge to authority, in creating densely metaphoric, politically suggestive figures.

Holy idiots and wise fools differ. Holy idiots are, traditionally, those who have mental defects but who also have mystical, visionary natures or at least unusual innocence and selflessness. Welsford gives as examples the Irish poet-seer/madmen and the medieval Arabian mendicant madmen who were revered as saints.[2] Wise fools, on the other hand, do not have visionary abilities, but along with their mental aberrancies they have considerable cleverness and wit: Shakespeare's fools are prime examples.

In both the wise fool and holy idiot traditions, then, characters with deficiencies are compensated by some mental or spiritual proficiency (second sight, wit). In Dickens's *Household Words*, the utilitarian Harriet Martineau ridiculed these elevated notions of idiots in an article entitled "Idiots Again," in which she proclaimed that it is not our business to cast out idiots or worship them but to try to reduce the number of children born idiots and make the most of the faculties of the idiots we have. In other words, she looked at these traditions as evasions of a harsh reality. Of course, in some senses she was right. The notion of idiots as holy, visionary, or witty can in part be attributed to a prevailing human desire to believe in divine justice and mercy—a universal optimistic impulse.[3] It is painful to accept that some people are born seriously deficient, so we devise notions of them being blessed in other ways. We read wisdom into their fragmented speeches, as Martineau pointed out in another, very similar *Household Words* article about deaf mutes:

> It was a sad misfortune to the class [deaf mutes] that the attempts . . . to retrieve their condition, were first made when men's minds were in a highly metaphysical condition, and they saw everywhere whatever they looked for, and could believe whatever they imagined. Hence arose the popular notion . . . that deaf mutes were a kind of sacredly favored class, cut off from vulgar associations, but endowed with an infinite soul, working purely in a kind of retreat from the world. The delusion was confirmed by the pretty poetical sort of things that the first pupils in the schools used to write, in pretty, broken language.

Far from seeing deaf mutes as blessed with elevated natures, Martineau depicts them as brutish: ". . . if the benevolent visionaries who repeated these things had lived five years with deaf mutes, seeing what was the arrogance and violence of their tempers, the childishness of their moods, and the astounding ignorance of the commonest things . . . the spectacle would have been a most bewildering one. . . ."[4]

Dickens, however, was typically opposed to such severely utilitarian views: after all, in the "Preliminary Word" of the first number of *Household Words* he proclaimed that the journal would defy the "iron binding of the mind to grim realities" and would "cherish that light of Fancy which is inherent in the human breast" (1). Although shrewdly realistic, Dickens prefers the fanciful, even the nonsensical. He who often textually affirmed a providential vision by his insistent use of coincidence and happy endings was no doubt in tune with the optimistic and perhaps unrealistic impulse to see some alternate blessing in those afflicted with mental or physical deficiencies.

Yet to suggest that the notion of holy idiots, wise fools, or poetical mutes springs solely from a desire for divine justice, from overzealous optimism, is to oversimplify the tradition and Dickens's own position. Idiots are characteristically oblivious to social norms, to ambition and responsibility, and to possessions. Their unworldliness calls into question the worldly ways that society considers acceptable and normal. They seem unconsciously to uphold a way of life more spiritual than that of the mainstream of society. Traditionally, holy idiots are more in tune with nature as well, perhaps because mentally they never leave childhood when sensibilities to nature are most acute. It is no coincidence that "natural" is another name for "idiot." Nature is alive and personified for the idiots of folklore, literature, and history; they seem to have a sense of "something far more deeply interfused," as can be seen particularly in Barnaby Rudge, who sees the world around him as possessed with spirits, and whose "enjoyment . . . [is] free and wild . . . in the face of nature" (*BR* 188; ch. 25). Even without supernatural visions or second sight, then, idiots share a "natural supernaturalism," an ability to see nature as miraculous and mystical.

The tradition of attributing mystical visions and prophecies to idiots stems in part from the fact that these figures lead such a marginal existence. Cut off from the everyday rituals that absorb those who are normal, the idiot has been seen as being more open to other senses that remain undeveloped in most people. Existing on the margins of "reality," the idiot would be more likely to see into an alternate reality, a spiritual level of existence, if anyone could.

The attribution of wisdom, or at least cleverness and wit, to fools both influences and develops from the roles they have played in society. Roman noblemen hired deformed eccentrics to ridicule them, partly in order to be entertained, of course, but also partly as insurance against misfortune. They felt that hubris could court bad luck—that the gods would afflict anyone who became too proud or too presumptuous; therefore, to prevent this from happening, they hired fools to mock them, thereby diverting "cosmic jealousy."[5] Shakespeare's fools work in a similar fashion. They are "all-licensed" critics who can ridicule the weaknesses of their masters with impunity. Wise fools naturally suggest an inversion of authority. Granted the right to make fun of those in power, those whom no one else can ridicule, the fool temporarily becomes powerful. The Feast of Fools, a medieval church festival that occurred around Christmas, emphasized the fool's capacity for inverting authority. On a particular day, laymen would dress up as clergy and hold mock services, imitating, often crudely, the voices and gestures of the local clergy. The festival provided the chance not only to ridicule particular authority figures but also to subvert temporarily the authority of the church itself. Commenting upon the fool's relation to authority, D. J. Gifford has suggested that the prime role of the fool has always been to bring into the order of society some of the anarchy society marginalizes, and to allow behavior that is usually not allowed.[6] Dickens's fools often function in a similar fashion, as shall be seen later.

Given the implications of the holy idiot and wise fool traditions, it seems that when Dickens provides his idiot characters with mystical visions he is upholding in the text a providential view of the world—a view that suggests that a benign authority is countering deficiencies with proficiencies. But more important, he is also questioning the basic norms of society and challenging authority through these types. The idiot and the fool are the absolute antithesis of the Victorian work ethic and strict norms of behavior. By celebrating the idiot, then, Dickens criticizes these standards. He also questions standard epistemological and ontological perspectives by celebrating those whose understanding of surface reality is scant but who, it has traditionally been supposed, seem to have a greater understanding of alternate realities. Of course, it is important to emphasize here, as I have in Chapter 2, that Dickens does not invest his nonfictional idiots with compensatory visions or wit, just the fictional ones. In his nonfiction, he can be as pragmatic in his approach to them as Harriet Martineau.

In his fiction, Dickens often uses physical details from the holy idiot and wise fool traditions to allude to early treatments and to symbolize the characters' epistemological and ontological perspectives. Historically, physical deformities are associated with fools. Enid Welsford points out that Romans preferred physical deformities in their fools; in the slave market the most deformed got the highest price.[7] In Russia it seems that grotesquely fat fools were preferred at the court of the czars.[8] In addition, some of the accoutrements of court fools and fool characters in festival plays imitate a physical deformity, for example, the cowl-shaped hood with ears and the cockscomb. Physical deformities helped separate the fool from those considered normal; the visual cues kept the boundaries safely demarcated.

But Dickens uses physical deformities for more than just demarcating his fools. He describes Smike, for instance, as having an "attenuated frame" and being "lame" (NN 79; ch. 7). Of course, on a literal level, his physical deformities are signs of the abusive treatment he received at Dotheboys, but they work in a more complex symbolic way as well. His "attenuated frame" suggests an image of being stretched too thin, of material being pulled to the point of transparency. The image is relevant; Smike has too little surface to cover too large an area. In typical holy fool tradition, then, he eschews surface and worldliness of any sort (not necessarily by choice in this instance), directing the attention to the insubstantiality of surface and to what lies beneath the surface. As he often repeats, worldly goods mean nothing to him; his only concern is being with Nicholas (NN 159; ch. 13). He is immaterial in both senses of the word—he has little "matter" to him, and he matters little, finally, in the bourgeois community the Nickleby's establish. It is also relevant that he is described as "lame," for he is, in fact, an extremely weak character, acted upon but rarely acting, except professionally with the

Crummles' troupe, and always needing Nicholas as a crutch. He cannot support himself economically and eventually not even physically. Finally not even Nicholas is able to keep him alive.

In the same novel, Newman Noggs, Ralph Nickleby's eccentric, fragmented, and often drunken clerk, is also marked by physical deformities that have symbolic value. Dickens describes him as a "tall man of middle-age, with two goggle eyes whereof one was a fixture, a rubicund nose, [and] a cadaverous face" (*NN* 8; ch. 2). Once again, the description has some very literal roots—the rubicund nose and perhaps the cadaverous face indicate Noggs's tendency to drink heavily. But the "two goggle eyes whereof one was a fixture" suggest some abnormality in Newman's vision. One eye stays rooted while the other can move. The image suggests an expansion of normal vision that is in tune with the visionary tradition of holy idiots, and indeed in his selfless devotion to the Nicklebys, Newman displays some of the "holy" traits of the holy fool. Of course the two views that Newman's eyes offer may result in mere chaos as well. Dickens provides Bunsby in *Dombey and Son* with a similar set of eyes, one fixed and the other revolving, and in his case the effect is to make Bunsby oddly detached from the scenes that surround him. The two-directional eyes suggest the potential for expanded vision, for an escape from the confines of a single perspective, but also suggest the anarchy of the idiot's view of the world. Perhaps for Dickens, heightened and anarchic vision are not contradictory but in fact closely related. Squeers is described as having only one eye, which of course suggests the opposite of the potential Newman's double vision gives him; Dickens links Squeers's uniscopic vision with stupidity and brutality (*NN* 30; ch. 4).[9]

Jenny Wren and Sloppy in *Our Mutual Friend* are other holy idiots distinguished by physical deformities that function as complex metaphors. Sloppy's body resembles Smike's "attenuated frame":

> Too much of him longwise, too little of him broadwise, and too many sharp angles of him angle-wise. . . . A considerable capital of knee and elbow and wrist and ankle had Sloppy, and he didn't know how to dispose of it to the best advantage, but was always investing it in wrong securities, and so getting himself into embarrassed circumstances. Full-Private Number One in the Awkward Squad of the rank and file of life was Sloppy, and yet had his glimmering notions of standing true to the Colours. (*OMF* 201; ch. 16)

As with Smike, Sloppy's deformities are a sign of his impoverished upbringing. But his physical awkwardness is also an outward indication of his social awkwardness, his inability to fit (even physically) into society. Dickens invokes the rhetoric of capitalism ("a considerable capital of knee . . . [which] he . . . was always investing . . . in wrong securities") to suggest that in such a system Sloppy is particularly unfit; in a society less based on material wealth, productivity, and normalcy, Sloppy might not always find himself in "embarrassed circumstances." In fact, the harsh poverty that is a by-product of capitalism is partly responsible for Sloppy's physical and social awkwardness, for he has had rickets, a disease caused by malnutrition, and his lack of social graces might easily be the result of his having been raised in the workhouse.

Jenny Wren's deformities are more debilitating. Dickens first describes her as a "dwarf," and Jenny herself frequently mentions that her "back's bad" and her "legs are queer" (OMF 222; bk. 2, ch. 1). Her face is described as "queer but not ugly" (OMF 222) and as looking "at once so young and so old" (OMF 224; bk. 2, ch. 1). Jenny's deformities seem opposite to those of Smike and Sloppy; instead of being attenuated, she is condensed and shrunken. Smike's attenuation suggested a kind of transparency, whereas Jenny's condensed and twisted frame suggests a complexity and compactedness that mirror the complexity of her psyche. Both holy idiot and wise fool, she has mystical, angelic visions along with biting, ego-deflating wit. She tells Lizzie and Eugene that sometimes she can smell flowers while she works even though there are none in the neighborhood, and she can hear birds sing and see white-clad children who come to comfort her (OMF 239; bk. 2, ch. 2); but her angelic visions are countered by her shrewish treatment of her father, her plans to browbeat the man who marries her, and her ridiculing of Eugene and Bradley. Even her call to "come up and be dead," which has an air of mysticism to it, has just as much morbidity (OMF 282; bk. 2, ch. 5).

As a dwarf Jenny Wren is an odd combination of young and old, since typically dwarves' faces mature while their bodies do not. So as a dwarf, she has an old-looking face and the body of a child. But Dickens tells us that even her face is a mixture, looking at once both "so young and so old." This mixture of youth and age in a holy idiot/wise fool character seems an odd, perhaps inverse, manifestation of the Romantics' (particularly Wordsworth's) call to keep the child alive in the adult. Jenny, who is both adult and child, is a freak; perhaps keeping the child alive in the adult is a positive goal, but a child forced to be adult is as unnatural as an adult trapped in childishness.

What is particularly interesting about Jenny's physical traits is that she is pretty in spite of her deformities. Dickens tells us that her face is "queer" but hastens to add "but not ugly" (OMF 222; bk. 2, ch. 1). Dickens seems reluctant to make female holy idiots and wise fools too grotesque, as he does quite happily with male fools. Perhaps he felt that it was not possible to make a female character appealing, positive, and ugly at the same time. Except for Maggy in *Little Dorrit,* Jenny is Dickens's most deformed, positive female fool, but he gives her long, beautiful, golden hair and bright eyes to compensate for her physical deficiencies. Fools such as Florence Dombey and Amy Dorrit, as shall be discussed in subsequent chapters, are restricted to norms of femininity and beauty, Florence having no physical abnormalities whatsoever. Dickens seems not to have been comfortable with much aberrancy in women, feeling, perhaps, that a woman who was too uncouth or too unattractive could not sustain readers' sympathies. With Jenny, Dickens departs somewhat from the strict limitations of femininity but not completely; he still partially yields to Victorian norms of female attractiveness.

Motley and absurdly ragged clothes are other elements that Dickens transforms from the holy idiot/wise fool traditions. Roman fools and dwarves, medieval and renaissance court fools, amateur fools of folk festivals, and even village idiots share certain similarities of dress, such as multicolored patches, which later developed into the more regular motley of court fools; odd and haphazard adornments, such as feathers, beads, and cockscombs; an odd mixture of styles; and often tattered and ill-fitting garments.[10] Dickens transforms this aspect of the tradition by mixing the rags of the mendicant with the elaborate motley of the court fool. What he gets is a costume, repeated in several variations, that is at once tattered and full of absurd adornments. The mixture accentuates the poverty of his fools while indicating that the clothes are not to be seen as merely the rags of a poor person.

Smike, for instance, wears a kind of motley suit, which is not just ragged but absurdly ragged. When Nicholas first observes Smike, he is surprised to see

> . . . the extraordinary mixture of garments which formed his dress. . . . he wore a skeleton suit, such as is usually put upon very little boys, and which, though most absurdly short in the arms and legs, was quite wide enough for his attenuated frame. In order that the lower part of his legs might be in perfect keeping with this singular dress, he had a very large pair of boots, originally made for tops, which might have been once worn by some stout farmer, but were now too patched and tattered for a beggar. . . . he still wore the same linen which he had first taken down; for, round his neck, was a tattered child's frill, only half concealed by a coarse, man's neckerchief. (*NN* 79; ch. 7)

Smike's clothes combine the child and the adult, just as did Jenny's face and body. He has a boy's suit and a man's boots, a child's frill and a man's neckerchief. The mixture symbolizes the innocence of the idiot even as an adult. He carries with him into adulthood the childlike view of the world, although he brings to adulthood little else. But the tattered garments are also emblematic of the holy idiot's denial of materiality and surface. " 'I want no clothes,' " Smike tells Nicholas when running away with him (*NN* 159; ch. 8). His denial of material goods indicates his other-worldliness. His tattered clothes, the broken surface he presents, and his attenuated frame suggest that as a holy idiot he sees past surface, through it or beyond it, and that whatever is beyond the surface might be glimpsed through him.

Newman Noggs's suit also suggests an incomplete surface; Dickens describes his clothes as being "much the worse for wear, very much too small, and placed upon such a short allowance of buttons that it was marvellous how he contrived to keep them on" (*NN* 8-9; ch. 2). Buttons seem to amuse Dickens. Sloppy and Toots have button problems too—Sloppy is "indiscreetly candid in the revelation of buttons; every button he had about him glaring at the public to a quite preternatural extent" (*OMF* 201; bk. 1, ch. 16), and Toots, at Dr. Blimber's party, fidgets with his waistcoat buttons to the point of distraction (*D&S* 96; ch. 14). Children often have difficulties with buttons; Newman's, Sloppy's, and Toots's button problems seem to emphasize that they are adult children. Also, since buttons are used to hold clothes together—in essence, to close up the gaps in the surface—it seems appropriate that characters who eschew surface, who speak what lies beyond surface, would have difficulties with buttons.

Barnaby Rudge's motley is more theatrical than Smike's or Newman's. His tattered green clothes are adorned with odds and ends such as "gaudy lace," "tawdry ruffles," "peacock's feathers," "parti-colored ends of ribands and poor glass toys" (*BR* 28; ch. 3). Dickens uses the word "motley" to describe Barnaby's costume: "The fluttered and confused disposition of all the motley scraps that formed his dress, bespoke, in a scarcely less degree than his eager and unsettled manner, the disorder of his mind, and by a grotesque contrast set off and heightened the more impressive wildness of his face" (*BR* 28). Here Dickens refers to clothes as speaking—"the scraps … bespoke … the disorder of his mind"—and he will continue to use clothes to indicate mental and spiritual states throughout the novel. Because of their theatricality, Barnaby's clothes draw even more attention to his fragmented and anarchic appearance than did Smike's or Newman's. And Dickens makes greater use of the implications of the broken surface in his portrayal of this figure. As I shall discuss in greater detail in Chapter 6, Barnaby's visionary nature, his ability to see past the surface of things, is upheld in the novel as being preferable to the static and worldly perspectives of the majority of society who are fixated on surface. Barnaby's tattered clothes, then, help to establish a dichotomy between surface and depth that becomes a central concern in the novel. Dickens also uses this focus on clothes and surface in general to allude to Carlyle's "philosophy of clothes," which suggests that one must be able to see beyond "clothes" in order to be wise.[11]

In addition to patched clothes, oversize and oddly shaped clothes and shoes are also a recurring element in the fool tradition, and Dickens picks up on this motif as a variation on his fools' tattered motley. The *Old Curiosity Shop*'s Marchioness, for instance, is first described as "a small slipshod girl in a dirty coarse apron and bib, which left nothing of her visible but her face and feet. She might as well have been dressed in a violin-case" (OCS 255; ch. 34). Her shoes are "extremely large and slipshod . . . [and fly] off every now and then" (OCS 484; ch. 65). Maggy in *Little Dorrit* also wears ill-suited (and ill-colored) clothing:

> A great white cap, with a quantity of opaque frilling that was always flapping about, apologized for Maggy's baldness, and made it so very difficult for her old black bonnet to retain its place upon her head, that it held on round her neck like a gipsy's baby. A commission of haberdashers could alone have reported what the rest of her poor dress was made of . . . (100-101; bk. 1, ch. 9)

The poorly fitting garments of these fools and idiots signify, as does Sloppy's awkward body, their inability to "fit" into society. They have no customary place—no real family, no family names, no money. Their clothes serve as badges for their placelessness, their homelessness, their unsuitability.

In general, by using allusions to the holy idiot/wise fool traditions, Dickens points to abnormal characters who used to have a place in society and often a highly respected role to play. Granted, some, perhaps even most, of the historic roles of idiots and the physically deformed were demeaning and exploitative. Undoubtedly the Roman fools were more laughed at than laughed with. And the fools used in early religious rituals were often used as scapegoats, so although they had a brief season of honor, the season often ended in death or banishment. But this was not always the case. Even when it was, at least they were valued to an extent for the very qualities that made them different instead of just punished for them or trained to imitate a very limited norm, as was the case in nineteenth-century asylum treatment. It is the limiting norm of Victorian society that Dickens criticizes most effectively through these characters, a norm that provides for only a very narrow range of acceptable behavior and appearance. Society, Dickens suggests, is diminishing itself by being too prudish to accept the aberrant. Of course, Victorians enjoyed viewing the insane and prisoners, but only as long as the subjects were behind bars or on a scaffold. Dickens overtly states his objections to this priggishness in the essay "Idiots," in which he addresses an imaginary, over-refined woman:

> . . . Madam, it were worth while to enquire . . . how much of the putting away of these unfortunates in past years, and how much of the putting away of many kinds of unfortunates at any time, may be attributable to that same refinement which cannot endure to be told about them. And madam, if I may make so bold, I will venture to submit whether such delicate persons as your ladyship may not be laying up a rather considerable stock of responsibility; and you will excuse my saying that I would not have so sensitive a heart in my bosom for the dignity of the whole corporation. (316)

But society does not segregate its abnormal members through prudishness alone. It does so, more importantly, out of fear. Idiots and madmen inspire fear because they threaten that which constitutes "society." As Enid Welsford remarks, "Under the dissolvent influence of [the Fool's] personality the iron network of physical, social and moral law, which enmeshes us from the cradle to the grave, seems—for the moment—negligible as a web of gossamer."[12] The fool, in other words, circumvents the "mechanisms of discipline" that provide for the normalization of individuals in society, thereby threatening the whole "carceral network" upon which society is based.[13] As suggested earlier, however, Dickens's female fools are less successful in circumventing disciplinary mechanisms because Dickens did not recognize the particular disciplines to which women were subject and was disturbed by the notion of threatening, rebellious females.[14]

But Dickens suggests that the holy idiot and wise fool are not the ones that society should fear and exclude. As Sandra Billington has pointed out, there are two diametrically opposed definitions of "fool" in the Bible: Psalm 13 characterizes a fool as a denier of god, a sinner, but Paul in I and II Corinthians suggests that Christians are seen as fools because of their selflessness and scorn for worldly matters.[15] Hebrew has two different words to signify these antithetical concepts of fools: one is "tam," which means "innocent fool"—one who has "no regards for material rewards"; the other is "ksl," which "contains the wilful, evil meanings of folly."[16] Therefore, in Judeo-Christian philosophy, a dichotomy is established between holy and, if you will, unholy fools. Dickens establishes a similar dichotomy in his novels, and by doing so suggests that the holy fool is an unfair victim of the fear that really should be felt for the unholy fool.

Dickens's unholy fools and madmen include criminals and other villains who experience visions or spells of insanity that are similar to those of the holy idiots but more fearful, and exhibit cleverness in ignorance as do wise fools. These characters include Fagin, who goes insane in the condemned cell, and Bill Sikes, who is haunted with visions of Nancy's face after he kills her (*OT*); Scrooge, who has more extensive communication with ghosts than any of Dickens's characters (*CC*); Carker with his prophetic and "visionary terror" in his flight from Dombey (*D&S* 767); Dombey, who experiences a complete mental breakdown after losing his wife and fortune (*D&S*); Bradley Headstone in his murderous madness (*OMF*); and John Jasper, whose opium hallucinations open *The Mystery of Edwin Drood* and whose hypnotic powers are alluded to several times in the uncompleted work. Through these characterizations, Dickens criticizes society for making greed the norm and the self-effacing, unworldly ways of holy idiots and fools abnormal. Society worships men like Dombey and Merdle who devote their lives to building financial empires. It courts these magnates, hanging on their every word, admiring those who have even a passing acquaintance with them. The dominant religion of English society may shun wealth and its trappings and bless the poor, but in practice, society despises poverty and applauds greed. The greed of men like Fagin, Ralph Nickleby, Jonas Chuzzlewit, Dombey, Carker, and Merdle directly leads to their downfalls and their fevered visions, spells of insanity, and suicides. Greed may be the norm, but it leads to some very abnormal visions and behaviors. The ethic that society implicitly accepts ends, for these characters, in a far more tragic isolation than that of the holy idiots and wise fools.

Scrooge offers a clear bridge between the unholy and the holy idiots. In the beginning of "A Christmas Carol," Scrooge is a devotee of Mammonism, a stubborn, unholy fool, but the visions that he experiences in the night—which are, as the ghost of Marley points out, a direct result of his own greed—transform him into a holy idiot on Christmas morning, laughing and prancing around his room. "I'm quite a baby," he exclaims. "Never mind. I don't care. I'd rather be a baby" (71-72). Converted to the childlike wonder and joy of the holy idiot, Scrooge leaves behind him the denial and greed of the unholy fool.

Ultimately, then, Dickens suggests that holy idiots and wise fools are marginalized because of their odd appearances and behavior, their spiritual visions, and their unworldly ways—all of which threaten the limiting norm and the network of power structures that made Victorian society possible. Yet the limiting norm supports a status quo that includes inadequate education, inadequate provisions for the poor, and a prevailing dedication to greed and reverence for the greedy, all of which are far more dangerous to the fabric of society than the unworldly ways of the idiot. Those who devotedly follow the norm often find themselves more marginalized and isolated than the abnormal, for it is the status quo that finally threatens society far more than any radical questioning of social institutions, practices, and beliefs could ever do.

NOTES

1. Dickens's knowledge of folklore has been well documented. Steven Marcus believes that "one of Dickens's chief qualifications among the novelists of the nineteenth century was his extensive and operative familiarity with the folklore and mythology of England and Europe..." (*Dickens: From Pickwick to Dombey* [New York: Basic Books, 1965], 155). Dickens's closest connection with the fools in Shakespeare came from his friendship with Macready, who played Lear in two productions that Dickens reviewed in the *Examiner*. (There is some dispute, however, over whether Dickens wrote the first review, which appeared on February 4, 1838.) The reviewer called the Fool "one of the most wonderful creations of Shakespeare's genius." And Butt and Tillotson (*Dickens at Work* [London: Methuen, 1957]), Lindsay ("Barnaby Rudge" in *Dickens and the Twentieth Century*, ed. John Gross and Gabriel Pearson [Toronto: Univ. of Toronto Press, 1962], 91-106), Marcus, McMaster (" 'Better to Be Silly': From Vision to Reality in *Barnaby Rudge*," *Dickens Studies Annual* 13 [1984]: 1-17), and others have referred to Dickens's allusions to fools in Wordsworth and Scott in his depiction of Barnaby Rudge.

2. Enid Welsford, *The Fool: His Social and Literary History* (Gloucester, MA: Peter Smith, 1966), 88-96; 78-79.

3. Harriet Martineau, "Idiots Again," *Household Words*, 15 April 1854: 197-200. Attributing heightened spirituality to idiots is also a result of primitive superstitions that often explained the unknown (in this case madness) by attributing it to the influence of supernatural forces.

4. Harriet Martineau, "Deaf Mutes," *Household Words*, 25 March 1854: 136.

5. Welsford, *The Fool*, 66.

6. D. J. Gifford, "Iconographical Notes Toward a Definition of the Medieval Fool," in *The Fool and the Trickster: Studies in Honour of Enid Welsford*, ed. Paul V. A. Williams (Cambridge: D. S. Brewer, 1979), 32.

7. Welsford, *The Fool*, 58.

8. Ibid., 185.

9. Dickens gives other idiot figures abnormal eyes. *Little Dorrit*'s Maggy is described as having only one eye as well. She is an idiot, but she is not given any of the compensating abilities of Dickens's holy idiots. Not only is her vision not enhanced in any way, it is actually limited. Her one good eye is just another deficiency. On the other hand, both Barnaby Rudge and Mr. Dick are idiots who are described as having prominent eyes. Mr. Dick's are "prominent and large, with a strange

kind of watery brightness in them" (*DC* 194; ch. 13); Barnaby's are "large, protruding eyes" with a "glassy lustre" (*BR* 28; ch. 3). In both cases, the physical descriptions emphasize their abnormal, heightened vision.

10. Welsford, *The Fool*, 78-79; 99, 122.

11. In *Dombey and Son*, Dickens deliberately inverts the clothes image by dressing the fools (Toots, Cuttle, and Bunsby) in elaborate, very complete outfits that present not only a solid surface but one that seems inseparable from the wearer. As I discuss in Chapter 7, Dickens inverts the image in *Dombey and Son* to explore a different aspect of Carlyle's clothes philosophy and also to call into question the alternatives the fool community offers.

12. Welsford, *The Fool*, 321.

13. Michel Foucault, *Discipline and Punish: The Birth of the Prison*, trans. Alan Sheridan (New York: Pantheon, 1977), 184, 209, 304.

14. Slater states that passion of any kind is what troubles Dickens in women:

> A frozen life, a premature death, a life selflessly devoted to others: such are the fates of Edith Dombey, Lady Dedlock, and Louisa Gradgrind. When we note that one or other of these fates is also allotted to nearly all Dickens's women characters who are endowed with passion we can register just how disturbed he was by this quality in the opposite sex; he seems compelled to show it as finally punished or at least neutralized. (*Dickens and Women* [Stanford, CA: Stanford Univ. Press, 1983], 265)

15. Sandra Billington, *A Social History of the Fool* (New York: St. Martin's Press, 1984), 45.

16. Ibid., 16.

Chapter 4

The Inarticulate

" 'Can't exactly say' won't do, you know."

—*Bleak House* 148; ch. 11

In *Bleak House*, the Coroner at the inquest concerning Nemo's death delivers the statement just quoted in reference to Jo, who is finally not allowed to testify because he "Can't exactly say" what will happen to him after he dies if he tells a lie in court. In this chapter I discuss a host of characters who " 'Can't exactly say' " much of anything and who are therefore segregated from society, imprisoned in their idiolects, as Jo is in this scene.

Inarticulateness is no minor problem for Dickens's characters. Their inability to communicate effectively, or at least standardly, isolates them in their private worlds with their private languages. Inarticulateness breeds isolation, and isolation, in turn, further exacerbates inarticulateness—a fact that not only hurts those isolated but the community from which they are isolated as well, as Charles Schuster points out:

> Language and society are functions in the same theoretical equation; each one exists as a value of the other. The Word is not just a naming, but a naming to someone else. Speech and communication depend on human contiguity—on physical, emotional, and intellectual touching. Conversely, society can only thrive or even exist when its members join together in a mutuality of ideas, experiences, felt values. . . . Language reaches out from one isolate to another and binds them together in a single, shared context. . . . Language makes society possible, and community is the sine qua non of speech.[1]

When an idiolect cannot reach out "from one isolate to another," or does reach out but is rejected, the speaker is left in solitary confinement, a prisoner to his or her own language, while society also suffers a loss, not as readily obvious but ultimately profound.

UNASSERTIVE AND NULLIFYING IDIOLECTS

Dickens characterizes the idiolects of holy idiots, wise fools, and other isolated figures with unassertive, even nullifying, taglines through which he emphasizes their marginal positions in his created worlds. He also suggests through these taglines how sociopolitical marginalization leads to imprisoning linguistic structures and how such structures lead to marginalization.

Unassertive idiolect patterns, such as taglines that repeatedly point out the inadequacy or unimportance of the speaker's words, or syntactical patterns that suggest a hesitancy to make an assertion, emphasize the self-doubt, humility, and marginalization of Dickens's idiots, madmen, and other prisoners.[2] The Marchioness, for example, frequently speaks in questions, no doubt fearing, after years of tyrannical treatment, to make any assertions. When Dick Swiveller first meets her he asks, " 'Why, who are you?' " to which her only answer is " 'Oh, please will you come and show the lodgings?' " (OCS 255; ch. 34) When Dick gives her a pot of purl to sample and asks " 'Well is it good?' " she responds, " 'Oh! isn't it?' " (OCS 427; ch. 57). Significantly, her penchant for questions decreases as she becomes closer to Dick and therefore less isolated.

Toots's verbal tag, "It's of no consequence," suggests a similar unassertive tendency. When Florence thanks him for being kind to her brother, he answers, " 'Oh, it's of no consequence,' " which is also his "invariable" reply to information concerning Florence's health, even though nothing really matters more to him (D&S 250; ch. 18, 315; ch. 22). When Carker asks Toots if he is hurt after Diogenes has attacked him, his reply is the same (D&S 317; ch. 22). Isolated as he is, Toots is of the opinion that nothing he says or feels is significant; therefore, his tagline acts as a kind of apology for his very existence. At Dr. Blimber's Academy, Toots was crammed with the sage pronouncements of the great authorities of Western thought until his brain short-circuited with the overload; the end result is his hesitation to make any assertion himself, to articulate his own feelings with any authority.

The unassertive verbal tag of Jo in *Bleak House* is, of course, " 'I don't know nothink,' " which he repeats frequently throughout the novel (220; ch. 16, 225; ch. 16, 648; ch. 47). The statement apologizes for his lack of knowledge and also implies that his ability to think ("nothink"= no think) is as deficient as his store of information.[3] Yet the double negative in his statement ironically makes the tag literally mean that Jo, in fact, does know something, a point that is emphasized by the narrator's comment that there "is something like a distant ray of light" in Jo's thinking (*BH* 152; ch. 11). On his deathbed, Jo modifies his tagline to " 'Never knowd nothink, sir' " (*BH* 648), which literally means that he always knew something, a fact that his characterization as a holy idiot points to throughout the novel. Jo, however, is only ever aware of his profound ignorance and marginalization, hence his repetition of his apologetic and self-effacing verbal tag.

Joe Gargery of *Great Expectations* tends to speak in dependent clauses, a syntactical pattern that complements his gentle and humble demeanor and his marginalized social status. Frequently he begins his dependent clauses with the tag " 'Which I meanter say,' " which not only suggests his hesitancy to utter *independent* clauses but also suggests that what he *means* to say is not always what comes out. In the following passage, for instance, Joe has told Pip that his sister is " 'Given to government,' " a phrase Pip understandably questions:

> "Given to government, Joe?" I was startled, for I had some shadowy idea (and I am afraid I must add, hope) that Joe had divorced her in favour of the Lords of the Admiralty, or Treasury.
>
> "Given to government," said Joe. "Which I meanter say the government of you and myself." (*GE* 44; ch. 7)

Joe's most concentrated display of this tag occurs in the scene in which Jaggers first tells Pip of his great expectations and offends Joe by trying to offer him money for the loss of Pip's services:

> "Now, Joseph Gargery, I warn you this is your last chance. No half measures with me. If you mean to take a present that I have it in charge to make you, speak out, and you shall have it. If on the contrary you mean to say—" Here, to his great amazement, he was stopped by Joe's suddenly working round him with every demonstration of a fell pugilistic purpose.
>
> "Which I meantersay," cried Joe, "that if you come into my place bull-baiting and badgering me, come out! Which I meantersay as sech if you're a man, come on! Which I meantersay that what I say, I meantersay and stand or fall by!" (*GE* 134; ch. 18)

It is interesting that Joe should use the tag so many times after being prompted by Jaggers's standard use of the phrase. Joe's abundant use of it here, in dealing with a lawyer, suggests that perhaps he considers the phrase part of legal terminology—and his assumption, in fact, is partly justified since Jaggers uses the phrase "mean to" and "mean to say" in close proximity and legal documents often do contain an abundance of "which" clauses. But Joe's nonstandard attempts to make his language sound more official only serve to point out his segregation from the class he imitates while subordinating his pronouncements in dependent clauses.

Not all of Joe's dependent clauses begin with "Which I meantersay"; some begin only with "which," as in the following scene where Pip first wakes up from his long illness to find Joe by his side: " 'Which dear old Pip, old chap,' said Joe, " 'you and me was ever friends. And when you're well enough to go out for a ride—what larks!' " (GE 439; ch. 57) Two of Joe's other tags, "Ever the best of friends" and "What larks!" are represented in this passage as well, working almost like a refrain, bringing back a familiar theme for Pip and the reader. But once again, Joe uses them in dependent clauses. Joe's idiolect has a crude expressiveness to it, but still his reliance on dependent clauses and other sentence fragments underscores his disconnectedness from and his humble position in Pip's world.

THE SILENT

"—the rest is silence."

—Hamlet 5.2.358

Silence has traditionally been a euphemism for death and "silencing" a euphemism for killing. But silence also has traditional associations with holiness and spirituality because prayer and meditation are usually conducted in silence, and "Christian" attributes such as meekness and self-effacement often entail silence. Dickens uses both of these associations in his character-izations of silent figures, but he emphasizes the connection between silence and death more forcefully and more often than the associations of silence and holiness. As was discussed in Chapter 2, Dickens believed that to be human a person must be able to communicate. Laura Bridgman, it will be remembered, is described by Dickens as inhuman before she learns sign language. The deaf, dumb, and blind girl in Lausanne is similarly described. Dickens's silent figures—those who are mute or who speak very little—most often appear inhuman or lifeless unless they are capable of some unspoken communication.

For instance, Sophy, a leading character in "Doctor Marigold," one of Dickens's Christmas stories, is a deaf-mute who appears subhuman before she is taught to communicate. Like Laura Bridgman and the deaf, dumb, and blind patients in Lausanne, she is first described as an animal.[4] Doctor Marigold thinks she looks as if "she had escaped from the Wild Beast Show" (CS 448). But he teaches her how to read and sends her to a school for the deaf and dumb. She never learns how to speak, but being able to sign and read, she can communicate and therefore establish relationships. She marries and has a daughter who is born without her afflictions. "The inarticulate illiterate has been franchised," Schuster writes in analyzing this story, "she has been taught to read, and her daughter is given the additional gift of speech."[5] In other words, Sophy has been given the chance to be human, to rise above the bestial.

Other Dickens mutes and near mutes emphasize more forcefully the connections between silence and death. Several of his women characters experience a period of muteness or near muteness that serves as a prelude to death. Mrs. Skewton, Mrs. Clennam, Mrs. Joe, and Miss Havisham all experience muteness before their deaths. Interestingly, their muteness also serves as a punishment for the ways in which they enacted their roles as mothers or mother figures. Mrs. Skewton acted as Edith's pander for years, but after her second stroke she is unable to continue her role, since she is left a "dumb old woman . . . crooked and shrunk up, and half of her is dead" (D&S 584; ch. 41). From silence, she sinks gradually into death. In *Great Expectations* Mrs. Joe is repaid for her terrifying Rampages by Orlick's attack, which leaves her partially deaf, dumb, and blind, although decidedly in a better temper. She too slips into death from this half-alive state. Miss Havisham's burning, which leaves her partially incoherent and eventually kills her, seems like a self-punishment since the accident occurs directly after she first recognizes her guilt in ruining the lives of Pip and Estella (GE 378-80; ch. 49). At first she is still capable of coherent speech after the incident, but gradually her repertoire of words sinks into three phrases that she endlessly repeats in the same order: " 'What have I done!' " then, " 'When she first came, I meant to save her from misery like mine,' " and then, " 'Take the pencil and write under my name, "I forgive her" ' " (GE 382; ch. 49). She speaks no other words for the remainder of the novel. Likewise, Mrs. Clennam's silence comes upon her as a punishment, as the narrator overtly tells us. After her house collapses, she too collapses, never again to move or speak a word (LD 794; ch. 31).

All four women, therefore, experience a period of muteness that is at once a prelude to death and a punishment for the ways in which they have lived their lives. The repetition of a hateful (or at least negative) mother figure finally and justly silenced suggests that perhaps Dickens vented some of his hostilities toward his own mother through these characterizations. He told Forster that he could never forgive his mother for wanting to send him back to the blacking warehouse when he was a boy,[6] and since he considered his mother garrulous—

she is the prototype for Mrs. Nickleby—he may very well have felt that muteness was a just punishment for her and any unnatural mothers like her.

Dickens portrays women who are silent by nature more favorably. The silence of Little Nell, Florence Dombey, and Amy Dorrit, among others, signifies their selflessness and therefore is depicted as something positive, even sanctified. Nell always has "something mild and quiet about her" (OCS 537; ch. 71), but she is never treated with more elevated and elaborate rhetoric than when she is dead and that quietness is permanent. Florence, in Dombey and Son, is also a silent martyr, her voice having been frozen within her by her father's coldness. But the silence of these women is not empty; often it serves as a reproach to ego. Amy, for instance, often tries to still her father's garrulous appeals for money with her own silent appeals. When her father tells Arthur about a particularly generous "Testimonial" he once received—hoping, of course, to elicit a similar offering from Clennam—Amy tries quietly to silence him: "To see her hand upon his arm in mute entreaty half-repressed, and her timid little shrinking figure turning away, was to see a sad, sad sight" (LD 83; bk. 1, ch. 8). Florence makes many such "mute entreaties" to her father in hopes of winning his affection. Her "speaking eyes, more earnest and pathetic in their voiceless speech than all the orators of all the world," make, we are told, a "mute address" to her father who greets them with his own silence (LD 503; ch. 35).

The silence of these women, although partially affirmed in the texts, is not depicted as entirely positive. Nell's silence, her selflessness, leads to her death. Florence's silence contributes to the gap between her and her father and allows her father's ego to grow unchecked; what he really needs is what he gets from Edith and Carker—a brutal challenge to his authority. Without it, he could not have had the rebirth that humanizes him. And Amy's silence leaves her a prisoner to her family's whims and to her own sense of the hopelessness of her love for Arthur. Only when she breaks out of silence and finds her own voice by telling Arthur of her love for him does she finally escape the prisons in which her silence has entrapped her. Dickens, therefore, serves out silence to punish his overly forceful female characters, while he partially affirms the silence of his docile women; yet he seems to recognize at least occasionally in these characterizations the dangers of women's silence, no matter how attractive it might be to him.[7]

Dickens makes strong connections between muteness and death in many of his silent male figures as well. Chuffey, for instance, rarely speaks—rarely even understands what is being said to him—unless Anthony Chuzzlewit speaks to him first. His silence makes him seem nonexistent:

. . . he sat down once more . . . and breathing on his shrivelled hands to warm them, remained with his poor blue nose immovable about his plate, looking at nothing, with eyes that saw nothing, and a face that meant nothing. Take him in that state, and he was an embodiment of nothing. Nothing else. (MC 178; ch. 11)

Jonas talks about him as if he were not even present. But when Anthony Chuzzlewit speaks to him, Chuffey comes alive and answers his questions. His replies may not be eloquent, but at least he is able to respond.

"Are you ready for your dinner, Chuffey?" asked the old man.

"Yes, yes," said Chuffey, lighting up into a sentient human creature at the first sound of the voice, so that it was at once a curious and quite a moving sight to see him. "Yes, yes. Quite ready, Mr. Chuzzlewit. Quite ready, sir. All ready, all ready, all ready." With that he stopped, smilingly, and listened for some further address; but being spoken to no more, the light forsook his face by little and little, until he was nothing again. (MC 179; ch. 11)

Because Merry is kind to him, she is able to develop the same rapport with Chuffey. As with most of Dickens's inarticulate characters, Chuffey needs to feel that he is part of a nonhostile community before he can communicate, even if it is only a community of two. When he faces the relentless criticism and ridicule of Jonas, he sinks back into muteness. It is necessary to speak to be considered human in Dickens's world, but it is necessary to be treated as human in order to speak.

Frederick Dorrit's near muteness shares many similarities with that of Chuffey. Like Chuffey, Frederick seems barely alive because of his silence. In the following description of Frederick in the theater, Dickens emphasizes the connection among silence, deafness, and death:

He had been in that place six nights a week for many years, but had never been observed to raise his eyes above his music-book, and was confidently believed to have never seen a play. There were legends in the place that he did not so much as know the popular heroes and heroines by sight, and that the low comedian had "mugged" at him in his richest manner fifty nights for a wager, and he had shown no trace of consciousness. The carpenters had a joke to the effect that he was dead without being aware of it; and the frequenters of the pit supposed him to pass his whole life, night and day, and Sunday and all, in the orchestra. . . . Some said he was poor, some said he was a wealthy miser; but he said nothing, never lifted up his bowed head, never varied his shuffling gait by getting his springless foot from the ground. Though expecting now to be summoned by his niece, he did not hear her until she had spoken to him three or four times. . . . (*LD* 236; ch. 20)

Although he is not abused as overtly as Chuffey, Frederick has been overwhelmed by his brother's verbosity and grand demeanor, as well as by their mutual misfortunes. He sees no point in trying to contribute to the conversation in his brother's commanding presence. William's criticisms of Frederick's sunken and silent state no doubt add to his desire to remain deep within himself. Granted, William's abuse is far more gentle than Jonas's abuse of Chuffey, but still William manages to deplete Frederick's confidence so that he rarely dares to commit himself to words.

But Frederick, like Chuffey, can rouse himself from his usual stupor in order to communicate with someone who treats him decently. The silence they keep, then, is not empty but full. In Frederick's case, Amy is the one with whom he can break through his isolation. Although he still does not speak much even with her, an unspoken understanding and affection exists between them, and they seem to enjoy each other's company. In the bustling society of Venice, Frederick and Amy are comfortable only in each other's society:

> He had insensibly acquired a new habit of shuffling into the picture galleries . . . and of passing hours and hours before the portraits of renowned Venetians. . . . After the first few days, Little Dorrit happened one morning to assist at these attentions. It so evidently heightened his gratification that she often accompanied him afterwards, and the greatest delight of which the old man had shown himself susceptible since his ruin, arose out of these excursions, when he would carry a chair about for her from picture to picture, and stand behind it, in spite of all her remonstrances, silently presenting her to the noble Venetians. (*LD* 481; bk. 2, ch. 5)

Unable or unwilling to speak much, Frederick seeks company in the silent Amy and in the mute portraits of society, perhaps feeling that in an atmosphere of silence, whatever nonverbal communication he is capable of might be better understood.

In *A Tale of Two Cities*, Dr. Manette is rendered virtually mute after almost eighteen years of solitary confinement. Manette's confinement and its consequent muteness are depicted as a kind of death, and his release from prison and his recovery are therefore a resurrection, as the first book, "Recalled to Life" indicates. Once again Dickens shows that for speech to be possible, the speaker must be part of a nonhostile community. Deprived of such a community, the speaker loses his ability to speak and eventually appears inhuman or lifeless.

Even Lucie refers to her father as an inanimate object when she first sees him: " 'I am afraid of it,' she answered, shuddering… 'I mean of him. Of my father' " (*TTC* 36; ch. 5). Manette barely speaks in this scene, and when he does his voice is strange and barely audible from lack of use.

> The faintness of the voice was pitiable and dreadful. It was not the faintness of physical weakness, though confinement and hard fare no doubt had their part in it. Its deplorable peculiarity was, that it was the faintness of solitude and disuse. It was like the last feeble echo of a sound made long and long ago. So entirely had it lost the life and resonance of the human voice, that it affected the senses like a once beautiful colour faded away into a poor weak stain. So sunken and suppressed it was, *that it was like a voice underground*. (*TTC* 38; ch. 5; emphasis added)

Manette's voice, in other words, has also been buried alive, and it cannot surface as quickly as he has. Manette slowly recovers from his near muteness when he is surrounded by his daughter and friends, but any time he is threatened, as when he discovers Charles Darnay's family connections, he relapses back into muteness. And he keeps silent about what he knows about Darnay—with one notable exception.

Chuffey, Frederick, and Manette all finally break out of their silence in protest or denunciation. This connection among silence, isolation, and revolt is an equation Dickens works out throughout his portrayals of imprisoned types, as I mentioned in Chapter 2. He suggests it in his nonfictional accounts of prisoners (*AN* 99), and he dramatizes it in many of his fictional characterizations. Human beings can stand only so much isolation, so much silence, before they rebel. Dickens's belief that silence leads to rebellion was no doubt influenced by Carlyle's pronouncements about rebellion in *Chartism*, which Dickens read in 1839.[8] Carlyle describes rebellion as the "gift of articulate utterance descending ever lower." In rebellions, he proclaims, "class after class not only acquires faculty of articulating what its might is, but likewise grows in might, acquires or loses might; so that always, after a space, there is not only new gift of articulating, but there is something new to articulate."[9] The rebellions of Chuffey, Dorrit, and Manette bring them "the gift of articulate utterance" and thereby a certain amount of power.

Chuffey finally emerges from his nothingness and stands up to Jonas to protect Merry:

> "If she has come to any harm," cried Chuffey, "mind! I'm old and silly; but I have my memory sometimes; and if she has come to any harm. . . . I won't bear it. I—I—have borne it too long, Jonas. I am silent, but I—I—I can speak. I—I—I can speak—" (*MC* 776; ch. 51)

Frederick Dorrit similarly breaks out of silence to defend Amy against the criticisms of William and Fanny. From his usual withdrawn quietude, he bursts forth with a long protestation against the family's pride and ingratitude, concluding with "I protest against any one of us here who have known what we have known, and have seen what we have seen setting up any pretension that puts Amy at a moment's disadvantage, or to the cost of a moment's pain" (*LD* 484; bk. 2, ch. 5). Dr. Manette's protest is more painfully ironic because it comes at a moment when he least wants to voice his objections to the injustices he has experienced. His protest—his outburst from muteness—is a document he writes as a solitary prisoner in the Bastille. In the paper he denounces the Evremondes and all their descendants "to the last of their race" (*TTC* 315; ch. 10). It is this paper, revealed years after Manette's release and restoration, that breaks the silence Manette has kept concerning Charles's family and leads the court to condemn Charles Evremonde, Manette's son-in-law, to death.

Other silent types in Dickens burst forth in protestations as well. Newman Noggs in *Nicholas Nickleby* and Twemlow in *Our Mutual Friend* may not be mutes, although they are very retiring, reserved, and often silent. Yet they break out of their molds in the end of their respective novels to finally make a stand. We are told that Newman "rarely spoke to anybody unless somebody spoke to him" (*NN* 9; ch. 2), but he becomes downright garrulous as he denounces Ralph Nickleby (so much so that his protestation seems false and awkward). Newman begins his denunciation by proclaiming " 'I *will* speak' " (*NN* 773; ch. 59), an assertion similar to Chuffey's " 'I—I—I can speak' " (*MC* 776). These declarations seem to help the near mutes finally find their voices.

Twemlow's protest is much more subdued and also more effective. He has spent a greater portion of the novel being baffled by the high company he keeps. Confused by the false intimacy and the artificiality of the society in which he moves, Twemlow usually remains silent. In fact, he is so silent that he is described as a piece of the Veneering's furniture (*OMF* 6; ch. 2). But at the end of the novel, Twemlow bravely contradicts the opinion of Society at a Veneering dinner, defends Eugene's marriage to Lizzie, and insists on calling Lizzie a lady. The protest is not vehement or dramatic, but it is firmly and bravely stated in contrast to popular opinion, quite a departure for Twemlow. The readers can particularly enjoy the denunciations of the wrongdoers in all these cases since they *are* departures—they come from the voices of those who have long been oppressed, repressed, or both, and who are finally getting a chance to vent their anger and frustrations.

Significantly, all the characters who break out of their silence to denounce the unjust are male, and all those who are silenced as a punishment are female. The woman as vehement protestor was not, apparently, a compelling figure for Dickens, perhaps because his view of women was limited by Victorian norms, which promoted, among other things, a demure and discreet silence for women. Women were supposed to be "quiet, virtuous, and immobile."[10] Silence for women was so celebrated that they were obliged "to 'kill' themselves . . . into art objects: slim, pale, passive beings whose 'charms' eerily recalled the snowy, porcelain immobility of the dead."[11] Consequently, silence in men often implied effeminacy—a lack of strength and a lack of will. Therefore, a man's emergence from silence in a vehement protestation was a real triumph. But a vehement woman was distasteful, unpleasant, and abnormal.[12] In fact, one of the traits that characterized women patients in insane asylums was their noisiness and their use of abusive language, which visitors found to be particularly shocking.[13] Dickens often remains entrapped in these traditional concepts of women. However, he does portray some strong-willed, outspoken women who are not necessarily distasteful—for instance, Edith Dombey, whose strong will is partially affirmed, although Dickens does quiet and seclude her at the end of the novel; Jenny Wren, whose strong will enables her to care for herself and her father; and Bella Wilfer, who rejects the doll in the doll house image. Helena Landless and Betsy Trotwood belong in this category as well.[14] Dickens at least tries to break out of the limiting norms set for women's behavior.

The Aged P is the most positively portrayed near mute in Dickens's fiction. He is almost completely deaf, and although he is not completely mute he relies more on nods and laughs than on words. Yet his silence and his deafness are not tragic. His son has provided him with a comfortable and entertaining home, and together with Miss Skiffins they form a pleasant community in which his communication deficiencies cause little or no problems. As a visitor, Pip is instructed by Wemmick to nod at the Aged P frequently; doing so, he pleases the old man and makes himself a comfortable, temporary addition to their extended family. The little forms of their everyday lives at Walworth serve as a kind of nonverbal communication as well—the flaps that drop open announcing the arrival of Wemmick and Miss Skiffins, the firing of the gun, the raising of the flag, the raising and lowering of the drawbridge.

With the Aged P, Dickens emphasizes the reverend quality of silence more than its deathlike implications. Wemmick's father seems almost hallowed in his fairy-tale home—a kind of allegorical figure of the beloved and respected parent. His name—the Aged Parent or Aged P—emphasizes his allegorical role. At the same time, his silence, broken chiefly through chuckles and nods, is reminiscent of the incoherent sounds of a happy, babbling baby. Once again Dickens, in portraying an idiot, emphasizes the child in the adult. Part of what makes the Aged P a reverend figure is his connection to childhood and particularly his use of the nonsensical language of childhood. There seems to be more worth in his chuckles and his incoherent speeches than in the sophisticated and elaborate rhetoric of more "adult" and "normal" types such as Jaggers and Pumblechook. Through the depiction of the relationship between Wemmick and the Aged P, a relationship vaguely reminiscent of that between Amy and Frederick Dorrit, Dickens suggests the possibility of meaningful communication without language, of the sanctity of silence. Silence, after all, does not have to suggest death. It can, although rarely, suggest the greatest kind of intimacy.

THE GARRULOUS

". . . a fool's voice is known by multitude of words."

—Ecclesiastes 5:3

Garrulousness was a quality with which Dickens was quite familiar. "Within his very family," Golding writes, ". . . Dickens was right from the beginning surrounded by extreme forms of eccentric verbosity, for each of his parents in their different ways shone in this respect, a fact confirmed both by report and by the idiolects of their fictional representations, Mrs. Nickleby, Mr. and Mrs. Micawber and Mr. William Dorrit."[15] But Dickens himself was garrulous; comic verbosity is one of the qualities that can be said to characterize his writing style. So he at once satirizes the loquacious while imitating them for comic effect.

While silence in Dickens has the somber overtones of sanctity and death, garrulousness is comic, riotous, and, as the quotation from Ecclesiastes suggests, foolish. Dickens's garrulous characters engage in absurd comic monologues, although, for the most part, they seem to be unaware of their absurdity. Ironically, the garrulous seem to be trying to form connections with their endless verbiage—connections between themselves and those around them, connections between their pasts and their presents, connections between their fantasies and their realities—but in most cases the more words they use in order to bridge these gaps, the greater the gaps grow. The effect is at once comic and pitiful, for the garrulous end up as isolated behind their walls of words as the silent, who rarely, if ever, speak. The garrulous, then, are ultimately silent, for their words are empty; paradoxically, as we have seen, some of Dickens's silent characters actually speak more clearly through their "mute entreaties" than do the loquacious with their many words.

Robert Golding explains the way in which the "never-ending" idiolect pattern short-circuits communication.[16] The idiolects of these characters

> . . . are characterised by an erratic and continual shifting away from the goal initially intended, this being often . . . utterly forgotten, each clausal shift adding more and more to the incongruity. This manner of speech delivery remains, in its illogical, garrulous wanderings, essentially the same for all of Dickens' loquacious personages, but in the latter works the never-ending patterns of such idiolects become increasingly intricate and disconnected.[17]

These characters talk as if words could fill the emptiness around them, or as if their words could transform the world, if they only used enough of them. But their attempts to fill or alter their worlds are usually just as futile as their attempts to make connections with their words—the more words they use, the emptier their speeches become. For them, more words mean less communication.

Mrs. Nickleby tries to bridge the gap between the past and present in her loquacious monologues. The changes in her financial, social, and marital status no doubt have left her feeling out of touch with her own history, so she tries to bring the past into relation with the present in her conversations. One of her first garrulous speeches demonstrates this. Ralph has just informed Kate and Mrs. Nickleby that he has procured for Kate a position with a milliner, and he tries to emphasize the advantages of the position by suggesting that many milliners become quite wealthy and even own their own equipages:

> "What your uncle says, is very true, Kate, my dear," said Mrs. Nickleby. "I recollect when your poor papa and I came to town after we were married, that a young lady brought me home a chip cottage-bonnet, with white and green trimming, and green persian lining, in her own carriage, which drove up to the door full gallop; —at least, I am not quite certain whether it was her own carriage or a hackney chariot, but I remember very well that the horse dropped down dead as he was turning round, and that your poor papa said he hadn't had any corn for a fortnight." (*NN* 120; ch. 10)

Mrs. Nickleby attempts to illuminate her daughter's present situation by invoking this scene from her past; unfortunately, the obvious application of this past experience is missed by Mrs. Nickleby. What her observation should have shown her, of course, is that the life of a milliner is far from lavish. But her confused narration of the experience focuses distractingly on minute details such as "green persian lining," details that emphasize her snobbery because they reveal that she concentrates primarily on items that indicate wealth and class. Because of her focus on such details, she misses the generalization that could have been derived from the experience. The monologue fails to connect the past with the present situation and therefore also fails to connect Mrs. Nickleby with her daughter, since Kate understands the implications of her mother's words more than her mother does. All of Mrs. Nickleby's attempts to bring the past into relation with the present end in similar confusion—she loses the points she tries to make, and she fails to communicate meaningfully with those around her.

Mrs. Nickleby meets her garrulous counterpart in the Gentleman in Small-clothes, who is as profuse with his words as he is with the vegetables he throws over the garden wall. The Gentleman in Small-clothes was formerly a mean-spirited tyrant who broke his wife's heart and turned away his children, but having gone mad he turns generous with his words, his vegetables, and his lovemaking. His keeper claims that it was his selfishness that turned him mad, as if his mind rebelled against the isolation his mean-spiritedness brought him. Yet his generous nature in madness leaves him isolated as well. He goes to great lengths to break out of his isolation— hurling vegetables, climbing garden walls, squeezing down chimneys, pouring forth verbiage—yet his methods are so eccentric and uncontrolled that he alienates himself even more, except of course from Mrs. Nickleby, who finds his verbal excesses quite comprehensible, as long as she is the object of his affectionate addresses. As with many of Dickens's garrulous, the Gentleman in Small-clothes produces an effect similar to that of a dam breaking: words pour forth uncontrollably, releasing built-up pressure caused by restraints. The Gentleman restrained or perverted natural human affection all his life until his dam burst; Mrs. Nickleby similarly restrained herself, although not, perhaps, as dramatically. Opting to fulfill social ambitions more than familial relationships, she thwarted a natural part of herself. Her flood of words is her uncontrollable answer to her contradictory impulses, yet it does not serve any useful purpose.

Sairey Gamp's garrulousness seems to be motivated primarily by a desire to establish connections with others—whether they are fictitious or factual others. Of course, establishing connections is part of her professional occupation. She is described as "a lady of that happy temperament which can be ecstatic without any other stimulating cause than a general desire to establish a large and profitable connexion" (MC 703, ch. 46). Golding implies that Sairey invents Mrs. Harris as a means of furthering her connections and promoting herself professionally,[18] but, although Sairey certainly does use her fictitious friend for this purpose, Mrs. Harris is much more than a professional ploy. How else can one explain the extensive and detailed creation of her by Mrs. Gamp? If Mrs. Harris were a straw woman invented only to be quoted in support of Mrs. Gamp's reputation, why would Sairey bother to give her such a varied and colorful background, as is demonstrated in the following quotation:

> "I knows a lady, which her name, I'll not deceive you, Mrs. Chuzzlewit, is Harris, her husband's brother bein' six foot three, and marked with a mad bull in Wellington boots upon his left arm, on account of his precious mother havin' been worrited by one into a shoemaker's shop, when in a stitiwation which blessed is the man as has his quiver full of sech, as many times I've said to Gamp when words has roge betwixt us on account of the expense—and often have I said to Mrs. Harris, 'Oh, Mrs. Harris, ma'am! your countenance is quite a angel's!' Which, but for Pimples, it would be. 'No, Sairey Gamp,' says she, 'you best of hard-working and industrious creeturs as ever was underpaid at any price, which underpaid you are, quite diff'rent. Harris had it done afore marriage at ten and six,' she says, 'and wore it faithful next his heart 'till the colour run, when the money was declined to be give back, and no arrangement could be come to. But he never said it was a angel's, Sairey, wotever he might have thought.' If Mrs. Harris's husband was here now," said Mrs. Gamp, looking round, and chuckling as she dropped a general curtsey, "he'd speak out plain, he would, and his dear wife would be the last to blame him! For if ever a woman lived know'd not wot it was to form a wish to pizon them as had good looks, and had no reagion give her by the best of husbands, Mrs. Harris is that ev'nly dispogician!" (MC 705; ch. 46)

Mrs. Gamp uses her abundant imagination and her abundant words to create an intimate and supporting friend for herself since the real world apparently has not offered her one. She may use her "relationship" with Mrs. Harris to promote herself professionally, but she also uses it to make herself feel less isolated, to make a very personal "connection" with someone else. Of course, her insistence on this fictitious character emphasizes her isolation by drawing attention to how involved she is in the workings of her own imagination. Sairey uses words to build for herself a world, one designed to her own needs. She authors her own reality, but she has apparently lost touch with the distinction between her fiction and reality.

Micawber and William Dorrit also attempt to author their own realities through their garrulous addresses. By using the speech of gentlemen, mixed with some polite poeticisms, they attempt to create the appearance of gentlemen in spite of their actual financial and social circumstances. Just as Micawber attempts to make his shabby clothes presentable by adding such adornments as "an imposing shirt-collar," "rusty tassels," and a useless "quizzing-glass," so does he adorn his speech with pseudogenteel embellishments:

> "Under the impression . . . that your peregrinations in this metropolis have not as yet been extensive, and that you might have some difficulty in penetrating the arcana of the Modern Babylon in the direction of the City Road—in short . . . that you might lose yourself—I shall be happy to call this evening, and instal you in the knowledge of the nearest way." (DC 156; ch. 11)

Unlike most of Dickens's garrulous characters, Micawber kindly offers a brief translation of his dense verbiage ("in short . . . that you might lose yourself"). He is not so involved in creating an impression that he will completely sacrifice communication. However, he fails to communicate the impression he intends to; only in his own eyes is he able to reshape his reality. Even the young David can see through the sham. The tawdry adornments on Micawber's clothes cannot hide his shabbiness—in fact, they accentuate it—nor can his embellished monologues make him a gentleman. His overblown speech indicates that he tries too hard to sound genteel and therefore gives him away. But his speech and his little adornments do help him build his self-image; they sustain his ego and enable him and his wife to recover quickly from their many depressing and degrading encounters with their creditors.

William Dorrit uses language more successfully to create the image of a gentleman, building around himself a devoted following at the Marshalsea solely by the power of his rhetoric and manners. But outside the Marshalsea his idiolect is less successful; he tries too hard, and the oddities in his speech hinder his attempts to fit into society. " 'Pa is extremely gentlemanly and extremely well informed,' " Fanny tells Amy in enumerating their social disadvantages, " 'but he is, in some trifling respects, a little different from other gentlemen of his fortune . . . partly, I fancy, on account of its often running in his mind that other people are thinking about [his imprisonment] while he is talking to them' " (LD 589; bk. 2, ch. 14). Dorrit's speeches become long-winded because of genteel phrases and euphemisms, self-justifications, attempts to solicit money without appearing like a beggar, and interjections of "ha" and "hem," which suggest that he undergoes some struggle with himself as he speaks. His following address to Arthur demonstrates these tendencies:

> "Amy, my dear, I have been trying half the day to remember the name of the gentleman from Camberwell who was introduced to me last Christmas week. . . . I mean . . . the gentleman who did that handsome action with so much delicacy. . . . it is almost a duty to mention it. I said at the time that I always would mention it on

every suitable occasion, without regard to personal sensitiveness. A—well—a—it's of no use to disguise the fact—you must know, Mr. Clennam, that it does sometimes occur that people who come here, desire to offer some little—Testimonial—to the Father of the place. . . . Sometimes . . . sometimes—hem—it takes one shape and sometimes another; but it is generally—ha—Money. And it is, I cannot but confess it, it is too often—hem—acceptable. This gentleman that I refer to, was presented to me, Mr. Clennam, in a manner highly gratifying to my feelings, and conversed not only with great politeness, but with great—ahem—information. . . . It appeared from his conversation that he had a garden. . . . it came out, through my admiring a very fine cluster of geranium . . . which he had brought from his conservatory. On my taking notice of its rich colour, he showed me a piece of paper round it, on which was written, 'For the Father of the Marshalsea,' and presented it to me. But this was—hem—not all. . . . I found that it contained—ahem—two guineas. I assure you, Mr. Clennam, I have received—hem—Testimonials in many ways, and of many degrees of value, and they have always been—ha—unfortunately acceptable; but I never was more pleased than with this—ahem—this particular Testimonial." (*LD* 84; bk. 1, ch. 8)

As I have suggested, Dorrit's loquaciousness is countered by Amy's "mute entreaties"; ironically, her silence conveys more than his many words do. Although both silence and garrulousness imprison speakers, Dickens shows garrulousness to be more isolating. The contradictions in Dorrit's speech and manner—his attempts to appear the gentleman and his unspoken realization of the falseness of his position—eventually culminate in his final, self-destructive monologue at the Merdle dinner where he has a breakdown and thinks he is back at the Marshalsea. This last, loquacious monologue completely alienates him from the society he so studiously cultivated with his gentlemanly speeches. His mind seems to revolt against his pretensions to fit into society, leaving him only with his pretensions about the honor of being the "Father of the Marshalsea" (*LD* 648; bk. 2, ch. 19).

Flora Finching tries bridging her past to her present, forming connections with others, and altering the reality of her circumstances through her loquacious monologues. Her constant references to her younger days when she and Arthur were in love indicate that she would like to connect the past and the present, which are so disappointingly different. Her own awareness of the great changes she has undergone adds to her verbosity, for she incessantly corrects the way she refers to Clennam, at once wanting to address him as she used to and yet feeling that to do so would be improper.

"In times forever fled Arthur," returned Mrs. Finching, "pray excuse me Doyce and Clennam infinitely more correct and though unquestionably distant still 'tis distance lends enchantment to the view, at least I don't mean that and if I did I suppose it would depend considerably on the nature of the view, but I'm running on again and you put it all out of my head." (*LD* 413; bk. 1, ch. 35)

Flora's speeches run into long-windedness partly because she cannot restrain herself from making romantic overtures to Arthur but cannot allow herself to do so uncensored, so she makes the overtures and then censors herself, as in the last speech where she flirtatiously refers to distance adding enchantment to the view and then immediately corrects herself, feeling that she has been too suggestive. Flora wants to express herself candidly, but she also wants to be socially correct. In trying to meet both desires, she runs into verbal labyrinths that fail to satisfy her own personal needs or the demands of decorum. Yet her monologues do allow her to play out little dramas, which fleetingly help her forget what she has become. Sometimes in the midst of one of her flirtatious speeches, she seems to have convinced herself momentarily that she is still attractive and that a romance between herself and Arthur is still possible (just as Micawber and Dorrit manage briefly to persuade themselves that they are who they are trying to be).

All of these garrulous characters at least temporarily draw attention to themselves through their extensive monologues, a fact that indicates that perhaps attention is, consciously or unconsciously, one of their motivations. But they fail to *hold* attention with their garrulousness, just as they fail to connect the past with the present, re-create their realities, or connect with others. They may gain the attention of others at first, but often they lose it because of their incomprehensibility. Other characters avoid talking to them for fear of inspiring more outbursts—Ralph Nickleby tries to prevent Mrs. Nickleby's speeches, Arthur avoids Flora, the Gentleman in Small-clothes is restrained by his keeper, and even Amy tries to restrain her father when he begins his speeches about "Testimonials." But the garrulous cannot help themselves. They are compelled to speak, and speaking often destroys what they set out to accomplish since they cannot sufficiently control their words. The one thing they do gain is a certain power; their "neverending" speech patterns monopolize conversations, even when the listeners try to ignore them. By speaking so much, the garrulous keep others from speaking, and thereby gain a little power. Inhibiting speech, as we have seen from reviewing the separate and silent prison systems, is a powerful coercive practice. By talking so much, the garrulous dominate the scenes they are in so that even though they sometimes make themselves unpopular and tedious with their loquaciousness, they have a certain command over their captive audiences, who are usually too polite—or too overwhelmed—to shut them up. Of course, the garrulous are not necessarily aware of their effects, nor do they necessarily want to have such effects. There is a certain desperateness in their speeches, as if they sense too keenly that silence suggests death and are therefore frightened of stopping their stream of words, of falling out of language, out of life.

The inarticulate, in general, then, are trapped in idiolects that hamper communication, while often being trapped in other ways as well—in prisons, workhouses, physical or mental defects, and their own self-imposed prisons. Their isolation often fosters their problematic idiolects, and their idiolects in turn foster their isolation. The relationship between marginalization and language, then, becomes a vicious circle. But the circle can be broken, Dickens shows us, by individuals and small communities that choose to understand those difficult to comprehend instead of choosing not to comprehend them. For, after all that has been said about the peculiar speech patterns of the inarticulate, what is truly surprising is how well they *can* be understood, in spite of their differences, as Amy understands her uncle, as Wemmick understands the Aged P, or Pip Joe. In the following chapters, I trace the course of imprisoned, inarticulate characters in four of Dickens's novels, demonstrating how Dickens suggests, first cautiously and then with greater assurance, the value of these figures to the community.

NOTES

1. Charles I. Schuster, "Dickens and the Language of Alienation," *English Language Notes* 16 (1978): 117.
2. Robert Golding in *Idiolects in Dickens* (London: Macmillan, 1985) points out that the famous comedian Charles Mathews greatly influenced Dickens's use of taglines (17-18).
3. Schuster, "Dickens and the Language of Alienation," 124.
4. Ibid., 125.
5. Ibid., 125-26.
6. Edgar Johnson, *Charles Dickens: His Tragedy and Triumph*, 2 vols. (New York: Simon and Schuster, 1952), 44.
7. These docile women are depicted as physically as well as verbally unimposing. They are all slight—Amy freakishly so, as shall be discussed in Chapter 8. As Susan Bordo states in "Anorexia Nervosa: Psychopathology as the Crystallization of Culture" (in *Feminism and Foucault: Reflections on Resistance*, ed. Irene Diamond and Lee Quinby [Boston: Northeastern Univ. Press, 1988], 87-117), "the female body ap-

pears...as the unknowing medium of the historical ebbs and flows of the
fears of woman-as-too-much" (108). Dickens's docile females tame
their words and their hungers so as not to appear "too much."

8. Jack Lindsay, "Barnaby Rudge," in *Dickens and the Twentieth Century*, ed.
    John Gross and Gabriel Pearson (Toronto: Univ. of Toronto Press,
    1962), 94.

9. Thomas Carlyle, *Chartism, Critical and Miscellaneous Essays*, vol. 4 (New
    York: AMS Press, 1969), 176.

10. Elaine Showalter, "Victorian Women and Insanity," in *Madhouses, Mad-
    Doctors, and Madmen: The Social History of Psychiatry in the Victorian Era*, ed.
    Andrew Scull (London: Athlone Press, 1981), 320.

11. Sandra M. Gilbert and Susan Gubar, *The Madwoman in the Attic: The Woman
    Writer and the Nineteenth-Century Literary Imagination* (New Haven, CT: Yale
    Univ. Press, 1979), 25.

12. Richard D. Altick, *Victorian People and Ideas* (New York: W. W. Norton,
    1973), 54.

13. Showalter, "Victorian Women and Insanity," 320.

14. Michael Slater, *Dickens and Women* (Stanford, CA: Stanford Univ. Press,
    1983), 272, 288-89.

15. Golding, *Idiolects in Dickens*, 3.

16. Golding suggests that Charles Mathews's character, Mrs. Neverend, is
    the precursor of Dickens's garrulous characters (ibid., 21).

17. Ibid., 21.

18. Ibid., 112.

Chapter 5

Nicholas Nickleby:
Idiocy and the Bourgeois

In *Nicholas Nickleby*, for the first time, Dickens presents an idiot as a major character. Through Smike, whose brains have been addled by physical and mental abuse at Dotheboys Hall, Dickens attacks the inhumane conditions of many Yorkshire schools; through Nicholas's treatment of Smike, Dickens also suggests an alternative way of dealing with idiots in general. As I have suggested, Dickens's critique of the increasing institutionalization and normalization of the aberrant often resembles Foucault's position on these matters. Dickens overtly articulates his suspicions about institutionalization in the essay "Idiots," also quoted earlier: ". . . it were worth while to enquire . . . how much of the putting away of these unfortunates in past years, and how much of the putting away of many kinds of unfortunates at any time, may be attributable to that same refinement which cannot endure to be told about them" (316). Forster points to Mrs. Trotwood and her care of Mr. Dick as an example of Dickens's belief that asylums need not be the only answer for idiots,[1] but Nicholas and Smike offer the same alternative. Smike, therefore, becomes a focus for social criticism in the novel.

Structurally Smike is significant because it is upon his introduction into the narrative that a sense of plot begins to unfold; although the novel continues to be episodic, it achieves a greater sense of unity at this point. He is central to the major plot developments: he unwittingly instigates Nicholas's violent departure from Dotheboys, which naturally sets in motion their further adventures; he inspires Ralph and Squeers's revenge plot, serving, in typical holy fool tradition, as a scapegoat for their revenge against Nicholas; and the posthumous discovery of his parentage serves as the central revelation in the resolution of the plot. As a foil, Smike is also important in the development of Nicholas's character; the overly refined Nicholas can often be overbearing (S. J. Newman calls him "an intolerable mixture of priggishness, naivety and condescension"[2]), but in his sympathy for Smike and his decision to take care of him, Nicholas partially redeems himself. On the one hand, then, Dickens seems to place Smike in a very significant position in the novel.[3]

At the same time, however, Dickens seems to resist this focus on Smike. His characterization is often overly conventional and lifeless—so much so that he seems to disappear from many of the scenes he is in. And once the Nicklebys are settled in their happy cottage, Smike is gradually filtered out of the picture. Finally, even the alternative treatment of idiots that is suggested through Smike seems to be retracted. But Smike's fate is only part of a larger, enervating movement toward normalcy that pervades *Nicholas Nickleby*.

Accompanying Smike is a host of other idiot characters, such as Newman Noggs, the Gentleman in Small-clothes, Lord Verisopht, and Mrs. Nickleby, whose bizarre appearances, fragmented or garrulous speeches, and grotesque or silly mannerisms energize the novel. Often, in fact, these idiots are much more vital than Smike, a type of *King Lear* "poor fool" without the wit. But Noggs, Mrs. Nickleby, the Gentleman in Small-clothes, and Lord Verisopht suffer a similar fate to Smike's. Either excised from the novel or gradually normalized, their energy evaporates by the end of the narrative. Looking at a broader range of characters, it becomes clear that the eccentric and grotesque in general are marginalized: the lively Crummles troupe is exported to America, Squeers is transported, Mr. Mantalini is sent underground.

Smike sets the pattern for the general movement toward normalcy. Marcus has suggested that Smike dies because Dickens wanted to show that there are some wounds that cannot be healed—that "the serious consequences of a bad childhood" could not be remedied even by the Nickleby's kind treatment.[4] But Smike seems to suffer more from his "happy" present than he does from his abusive past. After leaving Dotheboys, he recovers his spirits and strength, enjoying whatever small services he can perform for Nicholas. He even flourishes in the Crummles troupe. In his first acting role he is received with great success and proclaimed "the very prince and prodigy of Apothecaries" (*NN* 330; ch. 25), and later earns "great applause" for his portrayal of a tailor (*NN* 386; ch. 30). Smike begins to fade only when he joins the Nicklebys in their happy cottage. His immersion in this bourgeois and stable world slowly kills him.

Smike's failing health is due in part to his unrequited love for Kate, but that is only the most overt cause. The underlying cause has to do with his sense of his own inferiority—a sense that is exacerbated by the "pity" he receives from the well-intentioned members of the Nickleby community. In an environment where everyone seems to belong but him, he senses his own deficiencies more painfully than ever. Ironically, we discover *after* his death that, as their cousin, Smike did in fact belong to that community and had a claim on their affections and support. The "charity" they give him is no more than what one might expect from a close relation—certainly no more than what the Nicklebys expected from Ralph when they came to London. Yet, because Smike is never aware of his familial connection, and because the Nicklebys are unaware of his relation to them, Smike comes to feel as if he is an unfair burden. Knowledge of his relationship to them may not have increased his self-esteem, but it may have increased his feeling of belonging. It may also have undermined, at least partially, the tone of superiority they unwittingly take toward him.

The undermining of Smike's self-esteem by the Nicklebys begins before Nicholas brings him to live with his family. Nicholas cares for Smike and offers him protection, affection, and even a family, but he has a bad habit of emphasizing Smike's faults through his pity. It is bad enough for Smike to be abused by those he hates at Dotheboys, but it is more damaging for him to be pitied by those he loves. Clearly it is not enough for Smike to have friends; he wants to be useful as well. When he and Nicholas leave London together in search of work, Smike enumerates his marketable skills: " 'I could milk a cow and groom a horse, with anybody,' " he proudly states, but Nicholas chooses to ignore Smike's skills in his inchoate plan to find employment aboard some ship in Portsmouth (*NN* 272; ch. 22). Nicholas points out the uselessness of Smike's skills aboard a ship: " 'I am afraid they don't keep many animals of either kind on board ship, Smike, and even when they have horses, that they are not very particular about rubbing them down ...' " (*NN* 272). He tops this deflation of Smike's feeble pride with the patronizing comment " 'still you can learn to do something else, you know ...and if you fail, it shall go hard but I'll do enough for us both' " (*NN* 272). At least Squeers, for all his abusiveness, testifies to Smike's worth: " '... he's a handy fellow out of doors, and worth his meat and drink, anyway' " (*NN* 80; ch. 7).

Despite his apparent affection for Smike, Nicholas continues emphasizing Smike's deficiencies and ignoring his few proficiencies. When Smike questions Nicholas about his history, Nicholas replies, " 'it is a long story ... and one you would have some difficulty in comprehending, I fear,' " an unjustified comment, considering that although Smike has problems with book learning he never has problems understanding anything Nicholas tells him (*NN* 375; ch. 29). Moreover, Nicholas consistently tags Smike with humbling terms such as "poor fellow" and "creature"; the first time the two talk together at Dotheboys,

Nicholas calls him a "poor fellow" and the pity in his tone makes Smike cry (*NN* 96; ch. 8). Nicholas again calls him this when Smike runs away with him (*NN* 159; ch. 13). The appellation becomes so standard that by the middle of the book Nicholas calls Smike a "poor fellow," a "devoted creature," a "poor boy," and a "foolish, silly creature" all in the space of a page and a half (*NN* 442-43; ch. 35). Naturally Smike comes to think of himself in these terms, and he too refers to himself as a "poor creature" (*NN* 443).

Appropriately, this conglomeration of belittling terms serves as a prelude to Smike's introduction to the Nickleby "home"; it is this home that will make Smike even more painfully aware of his deficiencies, for there Nicholas's destructive pity is matched by that of Kate, Frank, and the Cheeryble brothers. Only Mrs. Nickleby seems to appreciate Smike for himself; ironically, it is her reaction that Nicholas is most concerned about when he brings Smike home. Smike seems to have a premonition of how his new home will affect him, for after Nicholas says that he is taking him home, Smike begins talking about death rather longingly, saying " 'In the church-yard we are all alike, but here there are none like me' " (*NN* 443; ch. 35).

Soon after Smike joins the happy cottage community, he begins to fade. Miss La Creevy is the first to notice the change and speaks to Kate about it:

> "I am sure that since he has been here, he has grown from some strong cause, more conscious of his weak intellect. He feels it more. It gives him greater pain to know that he wanders sometimes, and cannot understand very simple things. I have watched him when you have not been by, my dear, sit brooding by himself, with such a look of pain as I could scarcely bear to see, and then get up and leave the room. . . . Not three weeks ago, he was a light-hearted busy creature, overjoyed to be in a bustle, and as happy as the day was long. Now, he is another being—the same willing, harmless, faithful, loving creature—but the same in nothing else." (*NN* 487; ch. 38)

Echoing her brother's pitying tones, Kate's response to this description is " 'Poor fellow!' " (*NN* 487). Although it is clear that Smike's unrequited love for Kate contributes to his decline, it is only part of a larger syndrome. His love for Kate is so painful because he has such an acute sense of his unworthiness, his inequality, and his position as a charity case—a sense constantly enforced by the pity of those around him. The first night the Cheerybles come to the Nickleby cottage, for instance, everyone gets along splendidly; when they stroll in the garden, Kate and Nicholas walk with Frank, Mrs. Nickleby walks with Mr. Cheeryble, and Smike accompanies them, "joining sometimes one group and sometimes the other, as brother Charles, laying his hand upon his shoulder bade him walk with him, or

Nicholas, looking smilingly round, beckoned him to come and talk with the old friend who understood him best" (*NN* 566; ch. 43). The evening should have been a happy one for Smike, but he ends it in a passion of grief. No doubt the camaraderie of the evening has made him sense his own outcast nature all the more painfully. Even the two groups' beckoning him to join them emphasizes his own sense of not belonging—in other words, everyone but him falls neatly into a little group.

At Dotheboys, amid a ragtag assortment of outcast boys and the physically and mentally twisted Squeers family, Smike may have been abused, but he did not seem exceptionally abnormal. On the road, as a vagabond with Nicholas, he carries his weight with energy and cheerfulness, experiencing something like what Foucault describes as the "easy wandering existence" of madmen in the Middle Ages.[5] With the eccentric Crummles troupe, his natural oddities become assets to his roles, in typical wise fool fashion. But at the increasingly stable, normal Nickleby cottage, he knows he has no place. The Nickleby home functions like Pinel and Tuke's moral treatment for the insane—it turns his gaze inward and makes him ashamed of his abnormality. Just as the reformed asylums "no longer punished the madman's guilt . . . but . . . organized it for the madman as a consciousness of himself, and as a non-reciprocal relation to the keeper," so does the Nickleby household build Smike's self-consciousness and his sense of inferiority.[6] Foucault suggests that one of the techniques of the moral treatment was to put a mirror up to the patient's madness so that he might see it for what it is and denounce it. The Nicklebys, good intentions not withstanding, provide Smike with such a mirror. And when he does denounce his aberrancy, he denounces his very life. It is as if he does not have enough material left in him with which to piece together the kind of surface he needs to fit in. He therefore begins a process of self-marginalization, secluding himself in his room when Frank Cheeryble comes to visit. He wishes for death, believing, as he says when Nicholas prepares to take him home, that in the graveyard at least we are all equal.

The alternative treatment of idiots that Dickens first suggested when Nicholas took responsibility for Smike is retracted by this picture of the idiot, unable to function in bourgeois society, and of bourgeois society unable ever fully to accept the idiot. The bourgeois community's real attitude toward Smike becomes clear after he dies. Miss La Creevy refers to Smike's death as a "poor reward" for all that Nicholas had done for him (*NN* 792; ch. 61). The Cheerybles conclude that it was better for Smike to have died than to have lived. " 'Every day that this poor lad had lived,' " Charles Cheeryble affirms, " 'he must have been less and less qualified for the world, and more

and more unhappy in his own deficiencies. It is better as it is, my dear sir' "
(*NN* 797-98; ch. 61). Nicholas assures him that he has come to the same
conclusion. Of course they are right—every day that Smike had continued
living in the company of those who think he is better off dead he would have
been more and more unhappy.

Dickens appears to voice his own assessment of Smike through the
Cheerybles and Nicholas; he apparently believes, at least part of the time,
that Smike is better off dead, since he begins killing him off almost as soon
as he creates him. Perhaps Miss La Creevy's comment that Smike's death is
a "poor reward" for all that Nicholas has done can also be applied to Dickens,
who may have felt that after focusing so much attention on Smike, it was a
poor reward for his efforts to find him so dull. Of all his idiot characters,
Smike is the most lifeless. Some of the holy fool traditions are alluded to in
his characterization, but none is brought to life or fully developed. The
tattered clothes, for instance, are part of his description, but they denote only
a broken surface—there is not much depth beneath to be uncovered. Dickens
will use the tattered clothes of the holy idiot more successfully and thoroughly in *Barnaby Rudge*. Smike doesn't suggest an alternative reality as does
Barnaby. He is not visionary. Granted, he does have the prophetic dream of
the hook in the ceiling from which his father eventually hangs himself, but
this is his only claim to visionary status. Moreover, he is utterly devoid of
humor, a deficiency that limits him to the pathetic. He also has no distinguishable idiolect, which makes him particularly lifeless in a novel with such
memorable idiolects as those of Mrs. Nickleby and Mr. Mantalini. Smike
demonstrates the selflessness typical of holy idiots, but this trait alone cannot
sustain interest. Because of these deficiencies of characterization, Smike
virtually disappears in some scenes. For instance in the Snevellicci dinner
scene, we are told that Smike accompanies Nicholas, Miss Ledrook, and Miss
Snevellicci to the party (*NN* 388; ch. 30), and five pages later we are told
that he helps pick up Mr. Snevellicci from the floor (*NN* 393; ch. 30), but in
between there is no mention of him—he speaks no word, and the narrator
does not chronicle any reaction, action, movement, or look on his part—it
is easy to forget that he is even present.

With his lifelessness and pathos, Smike holds an interesting relationship
to the child protagonists in *Oliver Twist* and *The Old Curiosity Shop*, the novels
immediately preceding and following *Nicholas Nickleby*. Smike is an inept
Oliver who dies. He is a Little Nell, chased by an ogre to his death—only
the chase in his case does not have the sexual interest of Quilp's hunt for
Nell. As a dead Oliver and a sexless Nell, Smike dies before he dies. Dickens
creates pathos with him, but little more.

Even the more energetic and original idiots are erased in this novel, however. Lord Verisopht, to begin with the least interesting example, is at least given, unlike Smike, a distinguishable idiolect, the dull drawl of a lazy aristocrat (an idiolect later to be refashioned for Mr. Sparkler in *Little Dorrit*), which, along with his bug-eyed ogling of Kate and his soft-headed trust for Sir Mulberry Hawk, produces a few humorous scenes. But this idiot stands little chance in the company of the worldly Hawk, who kills him in a duel and flees the country. Lord Verisopht begins being erased even before he is killed, however. Dickens focuses less on his idiocy and more on his nobility as the tale progresses. In the 1867 edition, Dickens ceases referring to him as "Verisopht" and uses instead "Lord Frederick" starting with chapter 26, partly, as Robin Gilmour points out, because as he became more sympathetic—and less idiotic—the derogatory name no longer suited him.[7]

A far more successful idiolect is created for the melodramatic Mr. Mantalini, whose glossary of endearing terms includes "a little rose in a demnition flower pot" (*NN* 258; ch. 21), "my essential juice of pine-apple," and, in reference to himself, "popolorum tibby" (*NN* 428; ch. 34). As with the Gentleman in Small-clothes, to be discussed, Dickens invests more energy and imagination in this creation than seems to be warranted by his position in the narrative. After all, as far as the plot is concerned, Mr. Mantalini is unessential. Of course, this devotion to peripheral characters and scenes is characteristic of Dickens, but the tendency seems stronger in this novel than in later works, perhaps because the central characters and scenes offer too narrow an outlet for his imagination and energy. When he tries to invest them with the kind of energy he gives some of the peripheral characters, he creates the awkward melodrama of some of Nicholas's speeches to Ralph and Sir Mulberry Hawk.[8] Dickens does not "kill" Mantalini as he does Verisopht, but he does diminish him. In Mr. Mantalini's final appearance, he is stripped to his shirt-sleeves, toiling away in a laundry and being screamed at by an irascible woman who is unaffected by his creative endearments. His moustache and whiskers are no longer dyed, his flashy clothes are worn, and he shamefully covers his face when he sees Kate. To add to his diminished position, Dickens sets the whole laundry in a cellar in a "wretched" neighborhood; Nicholas and Kate must "descend" to see him (*NN* 820; ch. 64).

The Gentleman in Small-clothes is a far more flamboyant eccentric than Verisopht or Mantalini, but one who is also eventually excised from the text. With his "vegetable love" and vegetable language, the Gentleman in Small-clothes displays an energy and fecundity of imagery that represents what is best in this novel. In the Gentleman's monologues—a patchwork of

Mercutio, Puck, and the daily news—Dickens's imagination overflows like the stream of vegetables thrown over the Nickleby's wall. The Gentleman serves as a kind of temporary antidote to the Nicklebys' stuffiness; perhaps Dickens sensed that the Nicklebys' "wall" of pride and priggishness was becoming a little tedious and needed to be breached by some comic cucumbers. Or, as Michael Cotsell suggests, perhaps Mrs. Nickleby is partly responsible for this vegetal excess, having "exceeded the walled gardens of domesticity that her children are trying to build up."[9] Unfortunately, Dickens finally values middle-class decorum over this kind of "play," to use S. J. Newman's term, and the final description of the Gentleman shows him being led away "guarded" by Tim Linkinwater and Frank Cheeryble (*NN* 650; ch. 49); we are assured several paragraphs later that he has been safely "housed" and his "custodians" informed of his escape (*NN* 651; ch. 49). It is as if Dickens had taken the more uninhibited portion of his imagination into custody and summarily locked it away.

Newman Noggs undergoes a more systematic marginalization and then a reformation. When first introduced, Noggs is a fragmented, frequently drunken figure with the customary freakish appearance and ill-suited clothes of the idiot:

> He was a tall man of middle-age, with two goggle eyes whereof one was a fixture, a rubicund nose, a cadaverous face, and a suit of clothes (if the term be allowable when they suited him not at all) much the worse for wear, very much too small, and placed upon such a short allowance of buttons that it was marvellous how he contrived to keep them on. (*NN* 8-9; ch. 2)

His idiolect consists mostly of fragments and grunts interspersed with much silence, "as he rarely [speaks] to anybody unless somebody [speaks] to him" (*NN* 9). When he writes to Nicholas he apologizes for having forgotten grammar and suggests he has forgotten a great deal more through his misfortunes. In spite of his deficiencies and poverty, he is important to the Nicklebys—at least as long as they are in need of assistance. He helps Mrs. Nickleby and Kate set up their barren new home. He takes care of Nicholas and Smike when they arrive on his doorstep. He helps them all move into their cottage. But when their lives become more stable and bourgeois, he is left out of the little community. He is never mentioned as one of the regular visitors to the cottage. (The Cheeryble brothers, Frank, and Miss La Creevy make up the regulars.) When he finally is invited to join the little community at the dinner party finale at the Cheerybles', Newman is exactly what his name suggests: a new man. Gone is his eccentric speech, mannerisms and dress, his drunkenness, his faulty memory. He is now dressed "genteelly," and he tells Nicholas, " 'I am another man now, Nick,' " (*NN* 816-17; ch. 63). To emphasize Newman's acceptability, Dickens describes him later in the same scene as "subdued yet so overjoyed" (*NN* 817). Noggs needed to be a new man to fit into this finale of normalcy, and Dickens made him so. To further assure his audience that Newman deserves his position in the family, Dickens describes him in the penultimate paragraph of the novel as a "quiet harmless gentleman" (*NN* 831; ch. 65).

Mrs. Nickleby undergoes a similar quieting, curbing process as Dickens brings the novel to its restrained conclusion. Mrs. Nickleby is one of Dickens's most successful idiots mostly because of her absurd memory associations and her garrulous idiolect. The associations she makes in some of her longer monologues are not much saner than those of the Gentleman in Small-clothes:

> "Kate, my dear . . . I don't know how it is, but a fine warm summer day like this, with the birds singing in every direction, always puts me in mind of roast pig, with sage and onion sauce, and made gravy. . . . Roast pig; let me see. On the day five weeks after you were christened, we had a roast—no, that couldn't have been a pig, either, because I recollect there were a pair of them to carve, and your poor papa and I could never have thought of sitting down to two pigs—they must have been partridges. Roast pig! I hardly think we ever could have had one, now I come to remember, for your papa could never bear the sight of them in the shops, and used to say that they always put him in mind of very little babies, only the pigs had much fairer complexions; and he had a horror of little babies, too, because he couldn't very well afford any increase to his family . . ." (*NN* 529; ch. 41)

Mrs. Nickleby's absurd speeches, gullibility, and class consciousness are satirized throughout the novel, as is her inability to comprehend changes. Her understanding of her situation and that of her children is almost always completely wrong. She is easily swayed by Ralph's transparent attempts to win her favor, which makes it easy for him to convince her that Kate could make a prosperous living working as a milliner's assistant and that Nicholas has been guilty of wrongdoing at Dotheboys. She is equally unable to comprehend Smike's position when Nicholas first brings him home, and she asks Smike if he ever dined with an aristocratic family she knew in Yorkshire. Nicholas finds it difficult to make her understand Madeline's situation as well. But as Dickens draws the novel to its conclusion, he erases many of these traits in Mrs. Nickleby's character, so that by the end she has graduated from absurdity to dignity and in the process becomes almost faceless and voiceless.

As with Newman Noggs's change, Mrs. Nickleby's becomes most apparent in chapter 63, which describes the dinner at the home of the Cheeryble brothers. When Mrs. Nickleby first receives the dinner invitation, she immediately suspects that some surprises are in store for them, and of course she is right—the Cheerybles have their grand matchmaking schemes in the works. In the last chapter we find that her predictions about Nicholas becoming a partner eventually become true as well, so that Mrs. Nickleby, who for most of the novel is presented as misguided and foolish, suddenly becomes insightful and gifted with foreknowledge.

Nicholas teases his mother about her suspicions concerning the Cheeryble party, believing that nothing more than dinner will await them there; she answers his teasing by saying " 'I wouldn't be absurd, my dear, if I were you …because it's not by any means becoming, and doesn't suit you at all' " (*NN* 808; ch. 63). It seems she has decided that absurdity does not suit *her* at all, either, for her monologues noticeably diminish in size and scope at this point, and although she continues her silly superiority to Miss La Creevy, on all other points she becomes quite dignified, restrained, and normal. On the way to the Cheeryble dinner, she indulges in a reflection on past dinner parties she has attended, but significantly, Dickens does not give voice to this speech—he only tells us that she gave it, which naturally reduces its ludicrousness. At the dinner, Mrs. Nickleby is "grand and complacent" (*NN* 817; ch. 63), and she is "stately and distant" to Miss La Creevy (*NN* 818; ch. 63). Of course she has often before attempted to carry off the air of stateliness, but it has always been undercut by her absurd speeches; now, at the conclusion, since her speeches are fewer and shorter (when they are presented at all), she finally achieves a stately demeanor, which, of course, is much less interesting than her absurdity. In the concluding chapter, Dickens describes her finally as "always preserving a great appearance of dignity" (*NN* 831; ch. 65). He has not completely divorced her from her comical qualities by the end, but he has certainly normalized and restrained her.

Foucault's account of the "hysterization of women's bodies" provides a framework for interpreting Mrs. Nickleby's "progress" from absurdity to dignity. Mrs. Nickleby's normalization reflects her partial escape from and then re-entrapment in disciplinary mechanisms. In *History of Sexuality*, Foucault discusses how the family and the expectations of the "social body" are two forces through which women's bodies become disciplined—"qualified and disqualified"—to obey a sociosexual norm.[10] But the forces of family and society disintegrate for Mrs. Nickleby: her husband dies, she loses her social and economic position, her son leaves home, and her daughter goes to work. She no longer has a fixed habitation or position. But these upheavals give her a certain freedom. The flood of language she pours forth is just one effect of this freedom—she is freer sexually as well. She flirts with Mulberry Hawk, Lord Verisopht, and the Gentleman in Smalls, embarrassing Kate with her lack of decorum. As the novel closes, however, the structures of family and social class close around her again as Nicholas returns to the family, re-establishing a patriarchy and providing a stable home, income, and community of bourgeois friends. Mrs. Nickleby's language and behavior become more restrained as a result. One suspects that not only is Mrs. Nickleby more fun for readers earlier in the novel, but she is also *having* more fun in spite of (or because of) the hardships and uncertainties she experiences.

In *The Pickwick Papers* much of the idiocy and madness is relegated to the interpolated tales; in *Nicholas Nickleby* Dickens brings it to the foreground of the text, only to subdue or extricate it finally by the conclusion. Perhaps like a patient in Pinel's care, Dickens saw his own aberrancy held up before him in the form of his characters, and the images startled him, motivating him to re-establish normalcy. In *Barnaby Rudge*, he gives more life to the central idiot figure and more sustained energy to chaotic scenes and characters in general, yet the impulse toward normality still persists, as shall be shown later. As S. J. Newman points out, part of this impulse toward bourgeois normality could be due to Dickens's anxiety for society's acceptance: "*Nicholas Nickleby*, written concurrently with Dickens's acceptance by the fashionable world (he was elected to the Athenaeum Club in June 1838 and presented at Holland House in August), contains his most strenuous attempt to conform to the values of a society saturated by evangelicalism."[11] Dickens is just embarking on his career, and he knows he is being watched. The eye of Society is on him, and he is not yet successful or confident enough to challenge social decorum boldly. Still hypersensitive to slights, as he continues to be to a degree throughout his life, and anxious to put behind him his father's imprisonment for debt and his family's persistent economic precariousness, he opted finally for safe, middle ground in this novel.[12] It will take later novels for Dickens to create a world whose values seriously challenge the accepted values of mainstream society—a world in which idiots, madmen, and other prisoners can not only exist in society but thrive, perhaps even thrive more successfully than the bourgeois, not in spite of their abnormalities but because of them.

NOTES

1. John Forster, *Life of Charles Dickens* (New York: Hearst's, n.d.), 136.
2. S. J. Newman, *Dickens at Play* (New York: St. Martin's Press, 1981), 50.
3. Smike's importance was emphasized in the Royal Shakespeare Company's production of *Nicholas Nickleby*, in which Smike became the "central embodiment of suffering humanity," moving the focus of sympathy away from Nicholas and Kate and out to the poor. See Michael Cotsell, "Nicholas Nickleby: Dickens's First Young Man," *Dickens Quarterly 5*, no. 3 (1988): 124.
4. Steven Marcus, *Dickens: From Pickwick to Dombey* (New York: Basic Books, 1965), 121-23.
5. Michel Foucault, *Madness and Civilization: A History of Insanity in the Age of Reason*, trans. Richard Howard (New York: Pantheon, 1965), 8.
6. Ibid., 247.
7. Robin Gilmour, "Between Two Worlds: Aristocracy and Gentility in *Nicholas Nickleby*," *Dickens Quarterly 5*, no. 3 (1988): 117.
8. Michael Cotsell, "Nicholas Nickleby," 123.
9. Ibid., 125.
10. Michel Foucault, *The History of Sexuality*, trans. Robert Hurley (New York: Pantheon, 1978), 104.
11. Newman, *Dickens at Play*, 49.
12. Peter Ackroyd, *Dickens* (New York: HarperCollins, 1990), 98-99.

Chapter 6

The Conventional Idiot:
Surfaces and Signs in Barnaby Rudge

Many of the critics of *Barnaby Rudge* have commented upon how Dickens alludes to the holy idiot tradition through Barnaby, but most have stopped at naming the allusion, as do Steven Marcus, Juliet McMaster, and S. J. Newman.[1] Some critics hesitate even to discuss the title character however briefly.[2] Why has critical attention so often shied away from examining Barnaby, even though he is the title character? And why, when Barnaby is analyzed, is his connection to the holy fool tradition merely stated and not examined?

One possible explanation is that most critics have assumed, at least partially correctly, that Barnaby is a conventional holy fool character and, because conventional, therefore uninteresting as an imaginative creation. Critics point to Barnaby's predecessors in Shakespeare, Wordsworth, Scott, melodramas, and folklore in general. Very little of Barnaby is left that is not derivative, or so it would seem. Barnaby does, of course, embody many of the holy idiot traditions, and the conventions are handled too histrionically at times; however, this does not mean that Barnaby is unworthy of serious critical examination. The fact that Dickens chooses to make Barnaby so conventional is in itself worth examining. Moreover, exploring how Dickens uses these conventions can lead to insights into central epistemological concerns and curious structural patterns in the novel.

One of the conventions that Dickens uses in describing Barnaby is the motley and absurdly ragged clothes traditionally associated with fools and holy idiots.[3] As Enid Welsford has shown, and as I have discussed in Chapter 3, Roman fools, medieval and renaissance court fools, amateur fools of folk festivals, and even village idiots share certain similarities of dress such as multicolored patches that later developed into the more regular motley of court fools; odd and haphazard adornments such as feathers, beads, and cockscombs; and often tattered and ill-fitting garments.[4] Dickens uses shared elements of the tradition to create a costume that is at once tattered and full of absurd adornments that draw attention to the raggedness of the garments (*BR* 28; ch. 3).

The costume Dickens creates for Barnaby (and fool characters in other novels) emphasizes the other-worldly nature of the holy fool. Ragged clothes indicate the insubstantiality of surfaces by presenting surfaces with gaps. The idiots, it may be said, speak the gaps—speak what lies beneath the surface. Through their clothes and words they suggest a reality beyond the surface. Their clothes, then, are a figure for their mystical nature, which is another, perhaps the most important, holy fool convention. Because the holy fools customarily add tattered adornments to their costumes—in Barnaby's case, feathers and lace (*BR* 28; ch. 38), two of the most common accessories for the traditional holy fool—they at once draw particular attention to surface and to the fragmentation and fragility of surface reality.

Dickens's emblematic use of clothes in *Barnaby Rudge* seems to have been influenced by Carlyle, who, in *Sartor Resartus*, extensively develops the metaphor of clothes as surface, proclaiming the need to see beyond clothes, past surfaces in order to see a truer, more enduring reality.[5] The clothes of Barnaby, and of holy idiots in general, work as a similar metaphor; they are among many elements of the convention that make the holy idiot a figure for an "other" reality.[6] Throughout the novel, Dickens emphasizes the emblematic nature of the holy idiot/fool costume, extensively developing the clothes metaphor and the surface/depth dichotomy it establishes so that these images become entwined in the major theme, character, and plot developments.

Dickens develops the clothes metaphor and its surface/depth signification by alluding to specific passages from *Sartor Resartus* in some of Barnaby's speeches.[7] In a meeting with Chester, Barnaby draws Chester's attention to clothes on a line being blown about by wind:

> "Look down there," he said softly; "do you mark how they whisper in each other's ears. . . . Do you see how they stop for a moment, when they think there is no one looking, and mutter among themselves again; and then how they roll and gambol, delighted with the mischief they've been plotting. . . . I say—what is it that they plot and hatch? Do you know?... "
>
> "They are only clothes," returned the guest, ". . . hanging on those lines to dry . . ." (*BR* 81; ch. 10)

Barnaby's fanciful vision of the plotting and devious clothes is actually prophetic since he is in the presence of Chester, who is in the process of hatching plots. More important, however, Barnaby's vision alludes to Teufelsdrockh's declaration that the " 'beginning of all Wisdom is to look fixedly on clothes, or even with Armed eyesight, till they become transparent.' " [8] This is literally what Barnaby does when he stares at the clothes on the line and sees life within them or reads them as a sign of the secret plotting going on around him. He sees past their surface to something that they signify. When Chester tells Barnaby that he sees only clothes on the line, Barnaby responds with another Carlylean proclamation:

> "Why, how much better to be silly, than as wise as you! You don't see shadowy people there, like those that live in sleep—not you. Nor eyes in the knotted panes of glass, nor swift ghosts when it blows hard, nor do you hear voices in the air, nor see men stalking in the sky—not you! I lead a merrier life than you, with all your cleverness. You're the dull men. We're the bright ones." (*BR* 82; ch. 10)

Barnaby's sense of presences all around him is strikingly similar to Teufelsdrockh's philosophy of ghosts in the "Natural Supernaturalism" section of *Sartor Resartus*:

> The English Johnson longed, all his life, to see [a ghost]; but could not, though he went to Cock Lane, and thence to the church-vaults, and tapped on coffins. Foolish doctor! Did he never, with the mind's eye as well as with the body's, look round him into that full tide of human Life he so loved; did he never so much as look into Himself? The good Doctor was a Ghost, as actual and authentic as heart could wish; well-nigh a million of Ghosts were travelling the streets by his side. . . . Ghosts! There are nigh a thousand-million walking the earth openly at noon-tide . . . [9]

Barnaby shares Teufelsdrockh's sense of the abundant presence of spirits, although Teufelsdrockh's visionary proclamation is, of course, more self-conscious. [10] These allusions to *Sartor Resartus* vindicate Barnaby's irrational vision of the world; they suggest, as Foucault has written, that madness *is* knowledge. [11] Barnaby's vision is countered throughout the novel by characters whose vision never pierces surface realities; in fact, the rational, surface approach to reality is shown throughout the narrative to be limiting, even dangerous, and at least partially responsible for the long-unsolved murder and the riots.

On one hand, Barnaby's ability to see beneath the surface can be seen as merely conventional—the holy idiot traditionally has such gifts. But the convention as used in *Barnaby Rudge* is fundamental to the theme and structure of the narrative. Barnaby's gift is significant in a novel in which most of the characters are dangerously fixated on surfaces. Dickens develops the surface/depth theme throughout the novel by focusing on signs and how they are read. Sometimes the signs that are focused upon are signboards that proprietors hang out in front of their establishments to identify their businesses; Dickens draws particular attention to the Maypole, Golden Key, and Black Lion signs. Other physical phenomena are also emphasized as signs; for instance, Dickens continues the clothes metaphor by suggesting how clothes function as signs, and Michael Hollington in "Monstrous Faces: Physiognomy in *Barnaby Rudge*" has indicated how faces serve as signs in this novel as well.[12] But always the sign represents surface—it is the surface indicator or identifier that points to something larger than and beyond itself. As such, signs are limiting. For instance, clothes as signs are indicators of social class, even character, and therefore label and limit the wearer. Signs are also conventional, and conventions and traditions in this novel are shown to be suspect through such characters as John Willet and Chester, who are fixated on conventions and surfaces. Discussing Saussure's understanding of signs, Jonathan Culler writes that "all signs are arbitrary, involving a purely conventional association of conventionally delimited signifiers and signifieds."[13] Systems of conventions, in other words, are what enable signs to have meaning. Those who are fixated on signs seem also to be fixated on traditions and conventions; likewise, those who attempt to disrupt signs, in particular the rioters, tend to be motivated by a desire to disrupt the conventions and traditions that have limited and marginalized them.[14]

Dickens calls attention to signs in numerous passages that alone may seem of minor importance but that together suggest a major motif in the novel. In the first paragraph of the first chapter, Dickens describes the "emblem" of the Maypole Inn, a maypole made of a thirty-foot ash. Dickens begins the second paragraph of the novel with the words "The Maypole," and then qualifies the proper name with the clause "by which term from henceforth is meant the house, and not its sign" (*BR* 1; ch. 1), suggesting that it is important to distinguish the sign from its signified. Yet the rest of the first sentence of the second paragraph makes it quite clear which "Maypole" is being discussed. The whole sentence reads: "The Maypole—by which term from henceforth is meant the house, and not its sign—The Maypole was an old building, with more gable ends than a lazy man would care to count on a sunny day . . ." (*BR* 1). The qualifying phrase is unnecessary since the rest of the sentence clarifies that the building is being referred to, not the sign. Dickens draws attention to the sign in these two opening paragraphs in order to introduce a focus on signs and their arbitrary nature that he continues throughout the novel.

The Maypole's John Willet is fixated on signs, on surfaces in general. The conventional nature of signs no doubt appeals to him since he is so resistant to change and consistently refuses to acknowledge it. But the rioters violently rupture the Maypole sign when they attack the old inn. They saw down the sign and hoist it through the windows of the bar. The sign, in other words, impales the signified. This physical and linguistic disruption leaves Willet appropriately speechless. He never recovers from the shock of the attack (*BR* 633; ch. 82). But he regains at least a portion of his former comfortable position in his little community when he moves to a small cottage and plants "a fictitious Maypole" out front (*BR* 632; ch. 82). The sign, in this locale, signifies nothing—he is no longer an innkeeper. But he thinks he is still in business, and when he is provided with a slate on which to keep accounts, he fills it with fictitious records of his friends' purchases. The signs of his past profession—the Maypole and the slate—are the realities for him. So fixated on surfaces is he that surface alone becomes the only reality.

The Maypole is not the only sign affected by the rioters. Signs as indicators of establishments and conventions are natural targets for the mob. In fact, Dickens foreshadows the riots with several descriptions of disturbed signs. He twice describes signs as mournful, prior to the outbreak of the riots: "Some of the shops . . . still adhered to the old practice of hanging out a sign; and the creaking and swinging of these boards in their iron frames on windy nights, formed a strange and mournful concert for the ears of those who . . . hurried through the streets" (*BR* 123; ch. 16). Gabriel Varden's sign, the Golden Key, is also described as swinging with a "mournful creaking noise" (*BR* 32; ch. 4). The adjective "mournful" suggests that the signs are lamenting the passing of something, an appropriate image considering what happens during the riots. Dickens again foreshadows the riots when the five-year gap in the narrative ends with a description of a storm and its effects on signs: "A bitter storm of sleet . . . rattled on the trembling windows. Signboards, shaken past endurance in their creaking frames, fell crashing on the pavement . . . as though the earth were troubled" (*BR* 247; ch. 33). The increased violence in this description of the disturbance of signs (before they were "mournful"; now they are "shaken past endurance") indicates that the riots are much closer at hand. When the riots do break out, signs are demolished as foreshadowed. "The Golden Key itself, fair emblem of the locksmith's trade, [was] pulled down by the rioters, and roughly trampled under foot" much as the Maypole emblem is destroyed (*BR* 604; ch. 79). But Varden returns to his business, repaints his sign, and restores it to its proper place (*BR* 604; ch.

79). The restoration of the sign after the riots indicates that although the riots welled up from the depths of society and wrought much destruction on its surface, the damage they inflicted was only sign-deep. The system of conventions that produced the signs and enabled them to have meaning—the same system that repressed the "scum and refuse" that made up the rioters (*BR* 374; ch. 49)—is still intact.

Clothes that function as signs play a more central role in the novel. John Grueby judges that Barnaby is mad by looking at his clothes and other surface details (*BR* 436; ch. 57). Hugh is treated as an animal at least partly because of his tattered garments and unkempt appearance (*BR* 86; ch. 11), and John Chester is considered a gentleman of good character and wealth based on his fine dress and good manners. Such signs are often misleading. In chapter 1, Tom Cobb labels the stranger (actually Rudge) a highwayman, based on his ragged and weather-worn clothes, but Parkes corrects him, saying " 'Do you suppose highwaymen don't dress handsomer than that?' " (*BR* 6). Of course, Parkes is wrong—the stranger *is* a highwayman and a murderer besides. What makes this misreading of clothes-signs particularly important is that such a misreading is responsible for the Haredale murder remaining unsolved for twenty-eight years. It was assumed that the gardener murdered Haredale and Rudge, since the gardener was missing and Rudge's corpse was found at the bottom of a pond on the grounds. But the corpse was identified by using clothes as signs: " 'And far enough they might have looked for poor Mr. Rudge the steward, whose body—*scarcely to be recognised by his clothes and the watch and ring he wore*—was found, months afterwards, at the bottom of a piece of water in the grounds . . .' " (*BR* 14; ch. 1; emphasis added). Rudge was not the victim, of course, but the killer. But since those involved relied so heavily on clothes for identification, the wrong man is hunted as the murderer.

Because Barnaby sees beyond clothes, beyond signs in general, he is less likely to judge others based on their surfaces. For instance, he delights in the company of Hugh when no one else, besides perhaps Dennis, can. He welcomes Hugh back to the Boot, "patting him fondly on the back, as if instead of being the rough companion he was, he had been one of the most prepossessing of men" (*BR* 404; ch. 53). And Hugh responds to him with more warmth than he shows anyone else: " 'I'm a Turk if he don't give me a warmer welcome always than any man of sense,' said Hugh, shaking hands with him with a kind of ferocious friendship, strange enough to see" (*BR* 404). Barnaby's affection for Hugh is not sheer idiocy; he sees redeeming qualities in him that are actually there, although invisible to everyone else. Hugh's final speech before being hanged testifies to the fact that he genuinely cares for Barnaby and deeply regrets having involved him in any trouble; he declares that he would gladly give his life to save Barnaby's (*BR* 595-96; ch. 77). Barnaby's affection for him is not unwarranted. Hugh is what he is because too many have judged him by his rough surface and treated him consequently as an animal.

Barnaby's treatment of Hugh and the humanizing effects it has on him suggest that if more people could be as oblivious to surfaces as Barnaby, there would be less impetus toward violent riots and widespread destruction. Even Lord Gordon's obliviousness to surfaces seems laudable in this context; although his refusal to consider Barnaby mad is fostered partially by self-interest, and although his anti-Catholic diatribes suggest a different kind of fixation on surfaces, there is still some underlying wisdom in his warning, " '...we must not construe any trifling peculiarity into madness. Which of us... would be safe, if that were made the law!' " (*BR* 366; ch. 48).

Because most of the mainstream figures in *Barnaby Rudge* cannot see beneath surfaces and, in fact, violently defend the surfaces they have formed, the "scum and refuse of London" find their only outlet in rioting (*BR* 374; ch 49). Chester, an exemplary member of society, admired at court and eventually knighted, is metonymic for high society, which thereby suggests that all of his kind are as fixated on surfaces as he is. In describing Chester's ride to the Maypole, Dickens makes a generalization about how shallowly Chester and men like him read nature's signs:

> The thoughts of worldly men are for ever regulated by a moral law of gravitation, which, like the physical one, holds them down to earth . . . There are no signs in the sun, or in the moon, or in the stars, for their reading. They are like some wise men, who, learning to know each planet by its Latin name, have quite forgotten such small heavenly constellations as Charity, Forbearance, Universal Love, and Mercy . . . (*BR* 217; ch. 29)

Chester's fixation on surfaces is so strong that he completely denies the existence of depth:

> "The world is a lively place enough, in which we must accommodate ourselves to circumstances . . . be content to take froth for substance, *the surface for the depth*, the counterfeit for the real coin. I wonder no philosopher has ever established that our globe itself is hollow. It should be, if Nature is consistent in her works." (*BR* 91; ch. 12; emphasis added)

So enslaved to surface is he that he proclaims that he would have sent his own son away if he had turned out to be awkward or overgrown (*BR* 119;

ch. 15). Similarly, he refuses to acknowledge Hugh as his son due to appearances.

Those who are fixated on surfaces, who read signs literally and flatly, deny and repress those individuals and experiences that threaten the stability of their surface existence. As an idiot, Barnaby is a figure for all that is irrational, chaotic, and lawless—all that a stable society and a "normal" human mind must marginalize. Barnaby, restless and wandering, manages to evade the schedules and regimens—in Foucault's terms "the carceral network"—that give society structure.[15] He manages even to evade the law and the death sentence when at the last minute he is granted a full pardon for his crimes. Moreover, his visions are chaotic and disturbing.[16] Most of the characters seem unable to come to terms with such strange visions and impulses; if they have ever had such impulses, they have restrained them in themselves, and now they try to restrain them in others or marginalize those who cannot be restrained. John Willet, for instance, minimalizes chaotic creatures such as Barnaby and Hugh by proclaiming that they have no imagination (BR 82; ch. 10, 219; ch. 29). Chester refuses to accept the chaos and mystery that Barnaby represents by trying to eliminate it or by denying that it even exists. Characters like Barnaby, Chester believes, " 'make such very odd and embarrassing remarks, that they really ought to be hanged for the comfort of society' " (BR 574; ch. 75). The country gentleman, the brother of the Lord Mayor, expresses similar opinions; he feels that idiots like Barnaby should be locked up or executed.

The riots show, however, that chaos and irrationality cannot be long suppressed. Those whom society has tried most to repress—the lawless innocent idiots like Barnaby, the animalistic and uneducated masses like Hugh—rise up from the depths, tear down the signs that stand for all that has oppressed them, and make a mockery of the fragile veneer of civilization that society has established at their expense. According to Jack Lindsay, Dickens at least partially affirms the views of Barnaby and Gordon because they "represent the future striving to be born, the wild confusion of hopes and desires which can as yet be articulated only in the tones" of madmen.[17] Lindsay suggests that Dickens perceives revolution as Carlyle describes it in Chartism, as the attempt of a voiceless class to gain the "gift of articulate utterance."[18] Barnaby, Gordon, Hugh, and the mob they lead are all striving to find a voice by lashing out at the surfaces and conventions that have kept them mute and marginalized. Characters who insist on surfaces, who attempt to repress those who suggest the fragility of surface and the limitedness of rationality, foster the violence that can rise up to destroy them.

Thematically, then, Dickens seems to have created a novel in which fixation on surfaces and a limited normality leads to revolts, a novel in which irrationality and chaos are valued, to an extent, and stability and normality are suspect and superficial. But these implied values are undercut by the structure and the ending of the novel, which suggest different, contradictory values. Structurally, Dickens incriminates himself in the same exclusionary practices he damns in characters such as Willet, Chester, and the brother of the Lord Mayor. Dickens, too, oddly minimizes and marginalizes his "central" character. Barnaby is conspicuously absent from the six central chapters— the middle fifty pages—of the novel (chapters 39 to 44). He is absent from chapters 26 through 38 as well.[19] In a very literal sense, then, Barnaby is structurally decentered, marginalized. More important, however, Dickens also silences him in the conclusion of the narrative. Barnaby's last recorded speech is his words to Hugh as they are both about to be executed: " '. . . we shall know what makes the stars shine, *now!*' " (BR 595; ch. 77). Barnaby escapes execution, of course, but no further words of his are presented, even though forty pages of text remain and the speeches of Hugh, John, Joe, Dolly, Varden, Mrs. Varden, Emma, Edward, Chester, Haredale, and Miggs are presented after Barnaby's last words. Even Grip is silenced. "He was profoundly silent," we are told; "for a whole year he never indulged in any other sound than a grave, decorous croak" (BR 634; ch. 82). (After his year of silence, however, Grip does speak again, and his words are the last reported utterance in the book: " 'I'm a devil' " [BR 634].) Absent from the center of the novel and silenced at the end, Barnaby is scarcely less marginalized textually than he is in the society Dickens criticizes for its exclusionary nature.

In his treatment of Barnaby, Dickens seems to have bought into the bourgeois ethic, as described by Foucault, that "disobedience by religious fanaticism, resistance to work, and theft, the three great transgressions against bourgeois society . . . are not excusable, even by madness; they deserve . . . exclusion in the most rigorous sense of the term."[20] Barnaby is guilty of at least two of these transgressions, having participated in riots led by religious fanatics and having escaped the discipline of a regular work schedule due to his madness. If one includes destruction of property in a broad definition of theft, Barnaby is guilty of all three bourgeois sins. Dickens punishes him with narrative exclusion and restraint.

In addition to marginalizing Barnaby, Dickens minimalizes him by making him so conventional. I have indicated earlier ways in which the holy idiot conventions function in *Barnaby Rudge* to establish central themes. But because Barnaby is so thoroughly conventional, he lacks the power of some of Dickens's more imaginative idiot/fool figures such as Mr. Dick, Bunsby, Toots, Sloppy, and Jenny Wren. The holy idiot conventions are used in all of these characterizations, but these characters tend to have more individuality than Barnaby—they add to more than they mirror the conventions. As we have seen in this novel, conventions are suspect, and that includes Dickens's use of them. For example, the use of stock costumes to label Barnaby, Rudge, and Chester suggests that Dickens is as much fixated on surfaces as Willet or Chester. Dickens's use of these costumes asks the reader to "take the surface for the depth," to read the clothes as a sign of the character, even while he clearly criticizes such superficial readings.

Finally, the constraints of a happy ending lead Dickens to minimalize Barnaby even further. Barnaby's irrational nature, which in the context of a far too rational society seemed his greatest asset, becomes progressively more normal. "He became . . . more rational," the narrator cheerfully informs us, as if this change should be seen as a kind of "happy ending" for Barnaby, like the restoration of Esther's beauty in *Bleak House* (BR 633; ch. 82). Furthermore, the great expanse of Barnaby's wanderings is also limited: he refuses to go near London or even look upon it again. We also learn that he has become more useful and hardworking and never again leaves his mother. If this were an account of an employee, the news might be positive, but in the context of the novel, the changes seem much more of a loss than a gain.

Dickens chooses not to give voice to Barnaby's madness or even his increased rationality in the conclusion of the novel. Reason's dialogue with madness has been cut; in Foucault's terms, Dickens "thrusts into oblivion all those stammered imperfect words without fixed syntax in which the exchange between madness and reason was made."[21] Like Smike, Barnaby has experienced the "easy wandering existence" typical of medieval madmen;[22] also like Smike, Barnaby must exchange this life for a more stable, normal existence. Barnaby does not waste away as a result, as does Smike, but he seems to lose what he had to offer—to the community and to the reader.

Barnaby's history recapitulates the history of the treatment of the insane, as Foucault presents it in *Madness and Civilization*: the days of fairly unrestrained wandering, followed by a period of incarceration, followed by an attempted normalization that is as limiting and restraining as the physical incarceration. As Foucault suggests, this last stage is not a "liberation" as Pinel and Tuke suggested,[23] but a far more insidious chaining of the patient. Dickens's characterization of Barnaby bears out this analysis.

Dickens attempts, then, to write a novel in which the protagonist is an idiot and in which the qualities of irrationality and chaos represented by him are favored over society's overly rational surface of limiting signs. But Dickens's conservative impulses asserted themselves and left Barnaby decentered, minimalized, and finally silenced in spite of his position as title character. Perhaps Dickens struggled so long to write this novel (he wrote it over a period of five years—it was supposed to be his second novel, and instead it was his fifth) because he found it difficult to place a character like Barnaby at the center of a novel and have the center hold.[24] Dickens originally intended to entitle the novel *Gabriel Varden—Locksmith of London,* and perhaps, in the end, Varden, with all his generous, affable but bourgeois normality, and with his job as a maker of locks—a professional keeper of order—is more at the center of the novel than Barnaby. In *Nicholas Nickleby* Dickens was unable to envision an idiot in the unified community of his happy ending, so he discreetly removes Smike to the country and kills him off before reaching the conclusion. In *Barnaby Rudge* Dickens broadened his vision of the community to include the idiot, but still he must decenter, diminish, and finally silence him to make him fit.

NOTES

1. Steven Marcus, *Dickens: From Pickwick to Dombey* (New York: Basic Books, 1965), 191; Juliet McMaster, " 'Better to Be Silly': From Vision to Reality in *Barnaby Rudge,*" *Dickens Studies Annual* 13 (1984): 2; and S. J. Newman, "*Barnaby Rudge*: Dickens and Scott," in *Literature of the Romantic Period 1750-1850,* ed. R. T. Davies and B. G. Beatty (Liverpool: Liverpool Univ. Press, 1976), 185. Newman mentions Barnaby's connection with the holy fool tradition but believes Barnaby becomes a holy fool only in the scene in which he is almost hanged.

2. Although Edmund Wilson discusses *Barnaby Rudge* in "Dickens: The Two Scrooges," he never actually mentions Barnaby (*The Wound and the Bow* [New York: Oxford Univ. Press, 1947], 17-47). Marcus's influential interpretation of *Barnaby Rudge* leaves Barnaby oddly on the periphery of the novel that bears his name (*Dickens: From Pickwick to Dombey*). Barnaby is absent from Hillis Miller's discussion of *Barnaby Rudge* in *Charles Dickens: The World of His Novels* (Cambridge, MA: Harvard Univ. Press, 1965) and is again marginalized in other, otherwise fairly comprehensive interpretations of the novel. Jack Lindsay's and Iain Crawford's articles are exceptions; Lindsay focuses primarily on the inarticulate idiots and their essential connection to the theme of rebellion, as shall be discussed later ("Barnaby Rudge," in *Dickens and the Twentieth Century,* ed. John Gross and Gabriel Pearson [Toronto: Univ. of Toronto Press, 1962], 91-106), and Crawford carefully compares Barnaby and Wordsworth's Idiot Boy ("Nature . . . Drenched in Blood": *Barnaby Rudge* and Wordsworth's "The Idiot Boy," *Dickens Quarterly* 9, no. 1 [1991]: 38-47).

3. Barnaby's costume shares many similarities with the clothes of other fools/idiots in Dickens, such as Smike, the Marchioness, Maggy, and Sloppy.

4. Enid Welsford, *The Fool: His Social and Literary History* (Gloucester, MA: Peter Smith, 1966), 78-79, 99, 122.

5. In *Dickens and the Grotesque*, Michael Hollington briefly mentions but does not explore this connection ([London: Croom Helm, 1984], 104).

6. Dickens most likely named his title character "Barnaby" because the name means "son of prophecy," and thus helps further the connection between Barnaby and the visionary convention.

7. F. S. Schwarzbach argues that Dickens had read parts of *Sartor Resartus* as early as 1834 when it was being published in *Fraser's* Magazine ("Dickens and Carlyle Again: A Note on an Early Influence," *Dickensian* 73 [1977]: 149). It was not published as a book until 1838, but this is still three years before the weekly appearances of *Barnaby Rudge*. Carlyle and Dickens had met in 1840 (Johnson, *Charles Dickens: His Tragedy and Triumph*, 2 vols. [New York: Simon and Schuster, 1952], 316), but it is difficult to fix the exact date for Dickens's readings of his works. Goldberg attributes Dickens's increasing seriousness prior to leaving for the United States in 1842 "to having read Carlyle's writings" (*Carlyle and Dickens* [Athens: Univ. of Georgia Press, 1972], 6). It is at least very likely that Dickens had read *Sartor Resartus* by the time he began *Barnaby Rudge*.

8. Thomas Carlyle, *Sartor Resartus* (New York: Scribner's, n.d.), 67.

9. Ibid., 264-65.

10. Dickens seems to have shared Barnaby's sense of the ubiquitousness of spirits. On December 19, 1839, Dickens wrote a letter to Mr. Beadnell consoling him for the loss of his son, saying, "the air about us has been said to be thick with guardian angels, and I believe it, in my soul" (*The Letters of Charles Dickens*, Pilgrim ed., vol. 1 [Oxford: Clarendon Press, 1965], 620).

11. Michel Foucault, *Madness and Civilization: A History of Insanity in the Age of Reason*, trans. Richard Howard (New York: Pantheon, 1965), 21.

12. Michael Hollington, "Monstrous Faces: Physiognomy in *Barnaby Rudge*," *Dickens Quarterly* 9, no. 1 (1991): 6-14.

13. Jonathan Culler, *The Pursuit of Signs: Semiotics, Literature, Deconstruction* (Ithaca, NY: Cornell Univ. Press, 1981), 24.

14. Dickens underscores the conventional nature of signboards when he mentions that hanging out signs in front of businesses is an "old practice" (*BR* 123; ch. 16) and when he describes the Black Lion's sign by commenting that most depictions of lions on such signs are "conventional" (*BR* 234; ch. 31).

15. Michel Foucault, *Discipline and Punish: The Birth of the Prison*, trans. Alan Sheridan (New York: Pantheon, 1977), 304.

16. Interestingly, Barnaby's father shares many of these qualities with his son, although he functions as an "anti-Barnaby," demonstrating the negative side of what in Barnaby are positive qualities. Rudge, like

Barnaby, is lawless and wandering. Also like Barnaby, Rudge has visions—a keen sense of a reality beneath the surface. He tells Stagg that he was forced to return to the scene of his crime by the ghost of Haredale, and that every breath of air, every star, every flower spoke of the secret of his crime (*BR* 474; ch. 62).

17. Jack Lindsay, "Barnaby Rudge," in *Dickens and the Twentieth Century*, ed. John Gross and Gabriel Pearson (Toronto: Univ. of Toronto Press, 1962), 101.

18. Thomas Carlyle, *Chartism, Critical and Miscellaneous Essays*, vol. 4 (New York: AMS Press, 1969), 176.

19. Thelma Grove points out this absence in "Barnaby Rudge: A Case Study in Autism" (*Dickensian* [Autumn 1987]: 139-48). In explaining the absence, she suggests that Dickens had trouble writing a novel "whose hero is a mentally handicapped man" (139).

20. Foucault, *Madness*, 268.

21. Ibid., x.

22. Ibid., 8.

23. Ibid., 278.

24. John Butt and Kathleen Tillotson, *Dickens at Work* (London: Methuen, 1957), 76-77.

Chapter 7

Dombey and Son:
Favoring Foolishness and Chaos

In *Nicholas Nickleby* and *Barnaby Rudge*, Dickens established a pattern in which the mad, idiotic, and eccentric in general are gradually normalized or excluded as the novels progress. In *Dombey and Son*, he turns this pattern inside out. The division between sane and insane, normal and abnormal begins to dissolve in *Dombey and Son*.[1] The world of middle-class, mercantile ethics no longer seems sane, and the chaos and innocence that Dickens partly affirmed in *Nicholas Nickleby* and *Barnaby Rudge* are more fully affirmed here, as being far more humane and finally even productive. Dickens advances beyond confining folly to pathos, as he did in *Nicholas Nickleby* with Smike, and he makes it more positive than it was in *Barnaby Rudge*, where it was intertwined with the violent riots.

In *Dombey and Son*, through the railroad images, among others, Dickens suggests that chaos and its related folly, nonsense, and idiocy, are not necessarily antithetical to progress, to positive change. Dickens first describes the advance of the railroad as an earthquake, tearing through Staggs's Gardens, leaving behind a wasteland:

> . . . houses were knocked down; streets broken through and stopped; deep pits and trenches dug in the ground . . . . Here, a chaos of carts, overthrown and jumbled together, lay topsy-turvy at the bottom of a steep unnatural hill; there, confused treasures of iron soaked and rusted in something that had accidentally become a pond. Everywhere were bridges that led nowhere; thoroughfares that were wholly impassable; Babel towers of chimneys, wanting half their height... (*D&S* 62-63; ch. 6)

In spite of the destruction that the railroad creates, Dickens shows that out of the chaos comes positive change. Staggs's Gardens prospers from the disruption:

> ... the neighbourhood which had hesitated to acknowledge the railroad in its
> straggling days, had grown wise and penitent ... and now boasted of its powerful
> and prosperous relation. There were railway hotels, office-houses, lodging-
> houses, boarding-houses; railway plans, maps, views, wrappers, bottles, sand-
> wich-boxes, and timetables. .... To and from the heart of this great change, all
> day and night, throbbing currents rushed and returned incessantly like its life's
> blood. Crowds of people and mountains of goods, departing and arriving scores
> upon scores of times in every four-and-twenty hours, produced a fermentation
> in the place that was always in action. (D&S 218; ch. 15)

The railroad, like a heart, sustains the surrounding area, pumping life forces
throughout the body. Dickens sees in the image of the railroad the vital
potential in chaos, and his realization underscores the novel's spirit and the
importance of the characters who embody chaos in their idiocy and madness.

As an author, Dickens realized the importance of chaotic energy as a
stimulus to creativity. While working on *Dombey* in Lausanne in 1846,
Dickens felt that his creative energies were abated because of the absence
of the bustling motion of London: " 'the difficulty of going at what I call a
rapid pace is prodigious: it is almost an impossibility. I suppose this is partly
the effect of two years' ease, and partly of the absence of streets ...' "[2] He
took a trip to Geneva to rouse himself and found that " 'the sight of the
rushing Rhone seemed to stir [his] blood again.' "[3] Rush, motion, noise,
energy, confusion, and chaos fundamentally shape the creative process for
Dickens. It is natural, then, that he should emphasize the positive power of
chaos in *Dombey*.

In *Nicholas Nickleby* and *Barnaby Rudge* Dickens develops characters whose
normal and ordered lives offset the abnormality and chaos of his idiots and
madmen, and he establishes a similar pattern, at least at first, in *Dombey and
Son*. In *Nicholas Nickleby* he presents Nicholas as the epitome of bourgeois
normalcy, and he sets Smike and Newman (and others) against him as the
idiot foils. In *Barnaby Rudge* he establishes Gabriel Varden as the rock of
bourgeois normalcy; Barnaby, of course, is his foil. In *Dombey and Son* Dombey
and Carker and their sphere are the rigid bastions of normalcy and order.
Dickens sets against them the community of the Wooden Midshipman,
which includes, at various times, Sol Gills, Cuttle, Bunsby, Toots, as well as
Florence and Walter (whose positions in the community of oddity seem
honorary, as I shall discuss later). Moynahan refers to Dombey's sphere as
"heads without hearts" and to the Midshipman community as "hearts without heads," a phrase that emphasizes their holy fool natures and their
separation from rationality and order.[4] The dichotomy between these two

worlds is, therefore, similar to that established by Dickens in earlier novels. But in *Nicholas Nickleby* and *Barnaby Rudge* Dickens finally excluded or normalized the centers of nonsense that he originally celebrated, whereas in *Dombey and Son* he increasingly empowers these figures as the novel progresses, while diminishing or excluding the "heads without hearts."

The power of the "hearts without heads group" is developed gradually in *Dombey and Son;* for the first half of the narrative, it is Dombey and his sphere that seem to be more powerful and central, while the Midshipman group hovers on the margins of Dombey's world. In the beginning of the novel, Dickens depicts Dombey as being at the center of society—a symbol of bourgeois complacency, success, and normalcy. Major Bagstock describes Dombey as "paramount in the greatest city in the universe," which places him at the center of a great center (*D&S* 288; ch. 21). Dickens further develops Dombey's centrality by showing how the business world—and even the social world—revolves around him. Of course his home world, which includes his acquaintances and family, revolves around him as well, at least until Edith challenges his position.

The figures that embody chaotic, nonsensical force are first placed by Dickens on the periphery of Dombey's world in marginal social and economic positions. Their relation to Dombey's world suggests powerlessness, but Dickens gradually posits them as the center of a more profound force. Walter and Gills are first depicted as fairly powerless satellites in Dombey's universe. They have no part in the great fortune of Dombey's empire, and their dreams revolve around coming closer to Dombey's position. Their existence is meager; Gills has to go into debt to Dombey in order to avoid financial ruin. Walter appears to have no choice but to follow Dombey's orders to go to Barbados.

Socially, Walter and Gills, along with Cuttle and Bunsby, other members of the Wooden Midshipman community, are unacceptable to Dombey. The appearance of Cuttle and Walter at the Dombey breakfast table is a horror. The scene is a great comic set piece, with Dombey becoming increasingly affronted by Cuttle and Cuttle becoming more and more jubilant at the success of their mission. The scene demonstrates the two contradictory powers that Dickens establishes throughout the narrative. Clearly Dombey asserts his power in the scene; he has the money, and Walter and Cuttle have come to beg for it. Dombey tries to indoctrinate Paul into the love of power and money by letting him decide whether or not to make the loan: " ' ... you see, Paul ... how powerful money is, and how anxious people are to get it. Young Gay comes all this way to beg for money, and you, who are so grand and great, having got it, are going to let him have it, as a great favour and obligation' " (*D&S* 133; ch. 10).

Yet Cuttle unconsciously asserts his own power in this scene. His is the power of the child—the power that comes from a complete lack of self-doubt and self-consciousness and an obliviousness to the scorn and derision of others. His is the power of ignorance and nonsense:

> Captain Cuttle ought to have been withered by the look which Mr. Dombey bestowed upon him in acknowledgment of his patronage. But quite innocent of this, he closed one eye . . . and gave Mr. Dombey to understand by certain significant motions of his hook, that Walter was a little bashful at first, and might be expected to come out shortly. (*D&S* 130; ch. 10)

As collateral for the loan, the Captain proudly presents Dombey with his silver watch, teaspoons, and sugar tongs, just like a child trading marbles, a whistle, and baseball cards for a new toy. Walter, who does not have Cuttle's capacity for ignorance, is more subject to Dombey's influence. The breakfast scene leaves Walter "humbled and cast down" (*D&S* 135; ch. 10). But Cuttle cannot be humbled by Dombey; it is as if Dombey's power has no relation to Cuttle's world, and therefore it cannot subdue him. He leaves the scene believing that "the interview at which he had assisted was so very satisfactory and encouraging, as to be only a step or two removed from a regular betrothal of Florence to Walter" (*D&S* 135; ch. 10). What is so peculiar about his interpretation of the events is that he is at once both completely wrong and completely right. His interpretation of Dombey's actions is grossly inaccurate—he could not be more mistaken; yet he is also absolutely correct in assuming that the interview brings Walter and Florence one step closer to betrothal. His accurate prophecy in spite of his ignorance places him in the tradition of the prophetic holy fool.

Cuttle's physical appearance signifies a chaos that Dombey reacts to violently. Cuttle is both man and machine since his right hand has been replaced by a hook (" 'the—Instrument,' " as Miss Tox calls it [*D&S* 133; ch. 10]). Cuttle's conflation of the human world—the world of feeling—and the machine world is similar to the conflation of the two in the image of the railroad. The railroad is anthropomorphized: the Stagg's Gardens community comes to think of it as a "relation" (*D&S* 218; ch. 15), Dickens compares it to a "heart" (*D&S* 218; ch. 15), and Carker sees its "red eyes, bleared and dim" rushing toward him (*D&S* 779; ch. 55). Dickens's imagination, John Carey affirms, is most fully engaged in these types of figures that "are neither impersonal objects nor fully human," figures that "populate the border country between people and things."[5] They suggest disorder, a blurring of boundaries that naturally upsets the rigid, static Dombey: "[Cuttle] could not refrain from seizing . . . [Dombey's] right hand in his own solitary left, and while he held it open with his powerful fingers, bringing the hook down upon its palm in a transport of admiration. At this touch of warm feeling and cold iron, Mr. Dombey shivered all over" (*D&S* 134; ch. 10).

Cuttle's living quarters are another rich "border country." He lives in a lively boundary territory on the margins of land, in an area that seems to be part land, part water:

> Captain Cuttle lived on the brink of a little canal near the India Docks. . . . The gradual change from land to water, on the approach to Captain Cuttle's lodgings, was curious. It began with the erection of flag-staffs, as appurtenances to public-houses. . . . Then came rows of houses, with little vane-surmounted masts uprearing themselves from among the scarlet beans. Then ditches. Then pollard willows. Then more ditches. Then unaccountable patches of dirty water, hardly to be descried, for the ships that covered them. Then, the air was perfumed with chips; and all other trades were swallowed up in mast, oar, and block-making, and boat-building. Then, the ground grew marshy and unsettled. Then there was nothing to be smelt but rum and sugar. Then, Captain Cuttle's lodgings . . . were close before you. (*D&S* 116-17; ch. 9)

The Captain's area, like the Captain himself, defies definition, defies being fixed with the label "land" or "water." And like the country affected by the progress of the railroad, it is messy and disordered because of all the activity that goes on there. Its "unaccountable patches of dirty water" and "unsettled ground" are like the accidental ponds and undermined buildings of Staggs's Gardens. As we have seen, Dickens suggests that positive energy stems from such chaotic scenes.

Bunsby inhabits a similar amorphous territory. He lives on the margins of the sea, adrift in a boat, cut off from land to protect him from the tyranny of his landlady. When Florence and Cuttle go to visit him aboard the Cautious Clara,

> they [find] that cautious craft (which lay outside the tier) with her gangway removed, and half-a-dozen feet of river interposed between herself and her nearest neighbour. It appeared, from Captain Cuttle's explanation, that the great Bunsby, like himself, was cruelly treated by his landlady, and that when her usage of him for the time being was so hard that he could bear it no longer, he set this gulf between them as a last resource. (*D&S* 334; ch. 23)

Both men, it may be said, live on the edge, whereas Dombey appears to live at the center of the city and society in general; yet from the margins rises the community that ultimately becomes central in this novel.

Gills, Cuttle, and Bunsby inhabit psychological as well as physical borderlands. Gills always seems abstracted, as if he is never completely present mentally; Dickens describes him as "slow" with "a newly-awakened manner, such as he might have acquired by having stared for three or four days successively through every optical instrument in his shop, and suddenly came back to the world again, to find it green" (D&S 34; ch. 4). Yet Dickens affirms Gills's chaotic thinking by providing him in the conclusion with a small fortune earned through his haphazard investments and by portraying him throughout as the founder of the Midshipman community. Gills creates the atmosphere in which folly can flourish. He and Walter thrive on fanciful tales of storms at sea and shipwrecks. The "straining and creaking of timbers and masts" and "whistling and howling of . . . gale[s]" excite both of them, just as Dickens found chaotic scenes such as busy streets and rushing rivers invigorating (D&S 39; ch. 4). Gills and Walter seem to derive energy from mere stories of chaotic forces. Gills carries out his fancies by arranging his shop like a seagoing vessel, "everything . . . jammed into the tightest cases, fitted into the narrowest corners . . . and screwed into the acutest angles, to prevent its philosophical composure from being disturbed by the rolling of the sea" (D&S 33; ch. 4). The shop is a play ship, and the members of the Wooden Midshipman group are its play sailors; it is this fanciful territory that becomes the center for the community of nonsense.

Like Gills, Cuttle exists in a psychological borderland, rich with chaotic energies. As shown earlier, Cuttle has a certain power due to his innocence and ignorance. Even when he loses some of that innocence, Cuttle's fancy is depicted as a potent force—he creates a fairy tale for Walter and Florence and helps to provide a world in which that tale can come true. Like Gills, he fashions a world in which imagination can thrive.

But Cuttle's innocence and eccentric expressiveness also isolate him; he can usually communicate successfully within the parameters of the Wooden Midshipman community, but even there Dickens depicts him making incomprehensible signs to Walter— "waves and flourishes as nobody without a previous knowledge of his mystery, would have been at all likely to understand" (D&S 227; ch. 17). Outside the Midshipman community, Cuttle has as much if not more trouble reading the signs of others as he has in making his own signs comprehensible. He has no comprehension of Dombey's or Carker's opinions of him, and they find his nautical ramblings all but unintelligible. Dickens describes Cuttle in his lodgings on washing day as "cast away upon an island" surrounded by soapy water (D&S 330; ch. 23). By chapter 39 his physical isolation in that scene has been transformed into an even more severe social and psychological isolation. Walter and Gills have left, and his disenchantment with Carker has made him alienate himself from others as well. Dickens describes him as "self-buried" (*D&S* 542; ch. 39). When Rob the Grinder leaves him, his isolation is complete; Dickens continues the island imagery by referring to Cuttle as Robinson Crusoe (*D&S* 550; ch. 39). His own voice becomes strange to him.

Cuttle's experience, then, moves toward increasing entropy. The members of the Midshipman group disperse, drift apart, and the order of their everyday lives collapses. But out of this chaos comes the eventual regrouping of the Midshipman members in a rejuvenated, stronger community. It is as if an absolute upheaval of their world was necessary for them to progress to a new stage, to more powerful, self-determining lives. As with the railroad, chaos and destruction are necessary (even within the community of folly) before positive change can be produced.

Bunsby, the chief prophet-fool of the group, is even more drastically isolated from others and himself than Cuttle becomes. Far more abstracted than Gills, Bunsby never even looks at those he speaks to, he intersperses irrelevant interjections into conversations, and his prophecies are equivocal. Yet Dickens suggests that Bunsby has a certain power, and not just in Cuttle's opinion. His one stationary and one revolving eye suggest that his vision, in typical holy fool fashion, is heightened: he sees in more than one direction. His hair is also multidirectional, having "no governing inclination towards the north, east, west, or south, but [inclining] to all four quarters of the compass, and to every point upon it" (*D&S* 334; ch. 23). The image is at once chaotic and encompassing and underscores that Bunsby is ungoverned. In conversations, Dickens tells us, Bunsby appears to look more toward Greenland than toward anyone present, a comment that suggests abstraction but also farsightedness. The connotations of "Green-land" (in spite of the actual country) suggest that Bunsby's eye is turned toward fertile places, toward the Edenic. Bunsby's voice seems to come from somewhere else "quite independent of himself, as if he were possessed by a gruff spirit" (*D&S* 338; ch. 23). When he talks, it is "the voice" that speaks, not Bunsby. Of course, Bunsby *is* possessed by a spirit—the voice of Dickens. Dickens's sly reference to himself as a "gruff spirit" inhabiting one of his own characters elevates Bunsby's proclamations, which are punctuated with the inevitable, " 'the bearings of this observation lays in the application on it' " (*D&S* 338; ch. 23). The comment establishes him as the prophet of relativity. Nothing is known, nothing is set in Bunsby's world, and Dickens seems to affirm that view. Mentally (and even physically) Bunsby is the exact opposite of Dombey, the rigid, static man whose world and whose proclamations are fixed in stone. By making Bunsby a sympathetic holy fool, Dickens indicates that his chaotic vision and speech, no matter how nonsensical or equivocal, are superior to the fixed and stagnant world of Dombey.

Toots is another member of the Midshipman group who is isolated due to his idiolect, and yet who manages to regroup with the others in the conclusion. Although Toots is financially independent and has some claim to belong to fashionable society, he is perhaps more marginalized than any character in the novel. Having "blown" too soon, and realizing his ridiculous deficiencies in conversation, Toots does not court the high society that his financial independence might have led him to. Yet his money and social standing make him an odd man out in the Midshipman community as well, at least at first. The only person Toots can communicate comfortably with dies. He is trapped in greeting rituals. When he visits Florence after Paul's death he twice launches into a closed greeting, offering both the questions and the answers: " 'How d'ye do, Miss Dombey?' said Mr. Toots. 'I'm very well, I thank you; how are you?' " (D&S 250; ch. 18). Dickens captures his isolation most effectively by showing him engaged in writing letters to himself from famous people. Like his greetings, his letter writings are entirely self-contained. Yet Toots's greeting rituals are not completely unproductive; because he constantly greets—makes overtures of friendship—he finds for himself the connections he needs in the Midshipman community. In return, he brings within the ordered world of the Dombey household some of the disruption and emotion it so desperately needs. Florence, and eventually Cuttle and the rest of the Midshipman group, return Toots's greetings, giving him a community in which he can communicate.

The initial isolation of these characters and their exclusion from the world of Dombey is epitomized by an odd image directly at the center of the novel. The image appears in the central chapter of the novel and, in the Oxford Illustrated Dickens, on the central page of the novel as well. In *Dombey and Son*, chapter 31 is central thematically and structurally; it describes the events of the day of Dombey and Edith's marriage from pale, cold dawn to the pale, cold dawn of the next day. Dickens details the actions of Mr. Sownds the Beadle and Mrs. Miff the wheezy pew opener as they prepare for the wedding at the church. The significance of the wedding and their small office in it have made both of them feel self-important. Mr. Sownds complacently "suns his portly figure on the church steps, waiting for the marriage hour" (D&S 439; ch. 31). But Mrs. Miff expresses her importance more aggressively: "Truly, Mrs. Miff has cause to pounce on an unlucky dwarf child, with a giant baby, who peeps in at the porch, and drive her forth with indignation!" (D&S 439; ch. 31). This dwarf child and her monster baby make no other appearance in the novel but in this sentence, yet in their structurally central position and their symbolic resonance they become dis-proportionately important. They represent all the oddities, the abnormali-ties, the un-Dombeys who are systematically marginalized by Dombey and all of those—even Sownds and Miff—who temporarily gain importance via connection with Dombey. The dwarf child can be read as emblematic of Florence, who is consistently described as small of frame and who remains childlike in her innocence. The giant baby might symbolize Toots, Cuttle, or Bunsby—any of the childlike idiots with whom she associates, any of those who exist with her on the margins of Dombey's world.

But paradoxically, the giant baby could represent Dombey himself, for he is compared to his own baby in the first paragraphs of the novel and he remains in the infantile narcissistic stage throughout most of his adult life. By the end of the novel, he is reduced to the helplessness of a baby when he has lost his position of prominence, his mind, and his health. In an odd way then, it is Dombey and those influenced by his importance who exclude the Dombey figure in this grotesque little image. The paradox is appropriate, for as Dickens shows throughout, Dombey *does* alienate and isolate himself.

As central and powerful as Dombey appears in the first half of the novel, Dickens also suggests that even at the height of his influence, Dombey is impotent and isolated by his own manner. Polly thinks of him "in his solitary state, as if he were a lone prisoner in a cell, or a strange apparition that was not to be accosted or understood" (*D&S* 23; ch. 3). He sees himself as having been "quite shut out" from his wife's last moments (*D&S* 29; ch. 3). He is again shut out from his son's deathbed. "In all his life," Dickens tells us, "he had never made a friend" (*D&S* 47; ch. 5). For all his money and position he is powerless to win his son's affection or save his son's life. Dombey becomes a great emptiness at the heart of the novel. He is stripped even of his sense of self after he loses his wife, business, and fortune, so that when he looks in a mirror he sees not a person but an "it":

> Now it lifted up its head, examining the lines and hollows in its face; now hung it down again, and brooded afresh. Now it rose and walked about; now passed into the next room, and came back with something from the dressing-table in its breast. Now, it was looking at the bottom of the door, and thinking. (*D&S* 843; ch. 59)

Dombey, the bastion of normalcy, goes mad. The center that he inhabited collapses; at this point, the margins rush in to fill the vacuum.

The imagery used by some of the critics of *Dombey* is useful in visualizing this process of the center sinking and the margins rushing in. Tillotson concludes that Dombey's ruin shows that "prosperity [is] a house built on sand."[6] Moynahan refers to the idiot-community as being watery, because it is tearful and frequently associated with the sea, as opposed to Dombey who is dry, and "fears love as a death by drowning."[7] Combined, the two sets of images suggest that Dombey is like a figure on the shore of an island overcome by waves. An island—which has been central and powerful, dominant in the mercantile world—sinking and being overwhelmed by the waves that are its margins is an image that can be (and has been) seen as a warning of England's possible fate.[8] But the image also emphasizes Dombey's tininess in confronting the overwhelming forces around him. He is indeed a baby as he faces the big waves over which he has no power.

The "waves" that rush in to replace the sinking center are the members of the Midshipman community, who are the signs or voices of the deeper waves, the waves that bear away Mrs. Dombey, the waves that Paul hears speaking to him, all the subterranean, chaotic natural forces that destroy and create through destruction. For the most part, Dickens does not normalize these characters when he centralizes them in the conclusion; he maintains reason's dialogue with madness, a dialogue he cut in *Nicholas Nickleby* and *Barnaby Rudge*, as I have suggested earlier.[9] Gills still seems as befuddled as ever and his shop is still hopelessly behind the times, even though his investments have been successful. Cuttle is a little wiser in the ways of the world, but his seafaring idiolect remains, as does his unfounded belief in the Wooden Midshipman's importance in the world of trade and his tendency to break into song. Toots is able to converse more successfully by the conclusion of the novel, but he is still given to melodramatic turns of phrase and to misnaming Walter, Gills, and Cuttle.

Florence and Walter have no baffling idiolects, mental deficiencies, or behavioral aberrancies to be normalized. They are honorary members of the Wooden Midshipman community, not idiots in their own right. Although Moynahan describes Florence as "segregated from intelligence," he does not see her as belonging, by nature, to the Midshipman community; "she is the genius of the society rather than a dues-paying member."[10] Florence and Walter are linked to the nonsense of the Midshipman community by the fairy-tale imagery that surrounds them: the little, lost girl attacked by a witch; the boy lost at sea who returns a success; the beautiful young woman who marries her hero. Lyn Pykett emphasizes Florence's fairy-tale status, calling her a "Cinderella figure, the Beauty to Captain Cuttle's Beast . . . the Angel of innocence, the embodiment of transcendent goodness."[11] Appropriately, Florence gets inducted into the Wooden Midshipman's fairy-tale society when the witchlike Mrs. Brown strips off Florence's fine clothes and sends her back into the streets in the kind of motley rags in which Dickens usually dresses his fools.

Clothed as a fool, Florence is welcomed into the Midshipman community where she finds what seems to be a home. Florence and Walter are the prime beneficiaries of the chaos of the Midshipman community; the other Midshipman members are fairy godparents to them. Their marriage is the novel's image of closure, of happiness achieved, one of the positive changes brought about by the chaos and nonsense of the Wooden Midshipman community.

Florence's "honorary" membership in the Midshipman group raises an interesting issue. Dickens seems unable to create an eccentric heroine, one with the physical, mental, and linguistic abnormalities of male fools. Florence always speaks, acts, and looks like a proper lady, even when dressed in rags. Dickens subjects her to the traditional "disciplinary practices that engender the 'docile bodies' of women, bodies more docile than the bodies of men."[12] Such docility is necessary for her to be an attractive heroine, or so Dickens seems to think. By restricting Florence to Victorian norms of female behavior and beauty, Dickens partially excludes her from the chaos he has depicted as a powerful, creative force. She witnesses the chaos but does not contribute to it. He restricts her to the status of adornment in the Midshipman group and does not recognize that in some ways he does to Florence what Mrs. Skewton does to Edith or Mrs. Brown to Alice: he forms her to win approval and affection through traditional feminine charms. He seems to feel that Florence would not earn readers' affections if she were not pretty and proper, an unfair judgment of Victorian readers considering they took quite kindly to Charlotte Brontë's plain Jane the year after *Dombey and Son* was published. The scene in which Mrs. Brown dresses Florence in rags is the only departure Dickens allows Florence from strict norms of feminine attractiveness.

Beside Florence, the other members of the Midshipman community do not wear the typical motley clothes that Dickens used so often for his holy and wise fools (such as Smike and Barnaby) in earlier novels. In fact, Dickens turns the clothes imagery inside out in this novel, except in Florence's case, just as he turns the pattern of textual marginalization inside out. Florence wears rags in her introduction into the community, but the rest of the fools are described by Dickens as wearing garments that present a whole surface— sometimes even a hard and shiny surface—and in Toots's case, an elaborately tailored surface. Their clothes are so complete and solid, in fact, that they seem inseparable from the wearers:

> The Captain was one of those timber-looking men, suits of oak as well as hearts, whom it is almost impossible for the liveliest imagination to separate from any part of their dress, however insignificant. Accordingly, when Walter knocked at the door, and the Captain instantly poked his head out of one of his little front

windows, and hailed him, with the hard glazed hat already on it, and the shirt-collar like a sail, and the wide suit of blue, all standing as usual, Walter was as fully persuaded that he was always in that state, as if the Captain had been a bird and those had been his feathers. (*D&S* 117; ch. 9)

Later, Walter sees Cuttle's coat and waistcoat hanging out of the window at Brig Place, and is astounded that they can be separated from the Captain (*D&S* 208; ch. 15). Similarly, Bunsby seems to be made of the same material as his clothes. Dickens describes his face as "mahogany" and pays particular attention to the "massive wooden buttons" on his waistband (*D&S* 334; ch. 23). The rest of his clothes present an imposing surface as well with his "dreadnought pilot-coat" and his "dreadnought pilot-trousers" (*D&S* 334; ch. 23). Both Cuttle and Bunsby, then, are solid, and therefore reassuring. They can be knocked about, but they are durable.

Dickens also depicts Dombey as inseparable from his clothes, particularly in Florence's eyes. At her mother's deathbed, Florence looks over at Dombey and sees "the blue coat and stiff white cravat, which, with a pair of creaking boots and a very loud ticking watch, [embody] her idea of a father" (*D&S* 3; ch. 1). In another description, his body and his clothes seem to function together as a tool or machine, his head "turning . . . in his cravat, as if it were a socket" (*D&S* 53; ch. 5).

Of course Toots is the character most associated with clothes in this novel. He takes great pride in the elaborate creations of his tailors, Burgess and Co., and frequently makes them the topic of his conversations. In their first conversation together, Toots asks Paul who his tailor is, and later initiates another conversation by asking Paul if he is fond of waistcoats. At Dr. Blimber's party, Toots becomes completely absorbed in the way he is dressed:

> Mr. Toots appeared to be involved in a good deal of uncertainty whether, on the whole, it was judicious to button the bottom button of his waistcoat, and whether, on a calm revision of all the circumstances, it was best to wear his wristbands turned up or turned down. Observing that Mr. Feeder's were turned up, Mr. Toots turned his up; but the wristbands of the next arrival being turned down, Mr. Toots turned his down. The differences in point of waistcoat buttoning, not only at the bottom, but at the top too, became so numerous and complicated as the arrivals thickened, that Mr. Toots was continually fingering that article of dress, as if he were performing on some instrument; and appeared to find the incessant execution it demanded, quite bewildering. (*D&S* 196; ch. 14)

So absorbed in clothing is Mr. Toots that he uses problems in tailoring as a metaphor for his own inarticulateness: " 'You know,' said Mr. Toots, 'it's exactly as if Burgess and Co. wished to oblige a customer with a most extraordinary pair of trousers, and *could not* cut out what they had in their minds' " (*D&S* 785; ch. 56).

Since Dickens uses clothes in *Barnaby Rudge* as an allusion to *Sartor Resartus*, implying that Barnaby's tattered clothes symbolize his ability to see beneath surface, to " 'look fixedly on clothes until they become transparent,' "[13] what is to be made of Dickens's reversal of this image in *Dombey and Son?* In this novel it seems as if the idiot characters themselves have been turned inside out, as if their insides were their outsides. One might say that they wear their hearts on their sleeves, except that for Cuttle and Toots, at least, it would be more accurate to say their hearts *are* their sleeves. But certainly Dombey's clothes cannot be interpreted in the same way as those of Cuttle, Bunsby, and Toots. The difference seems to be that Dombey's clothes function as a kind of mask that he hides behind, whereas the clothes of Cuttle, Bunsby, and Toots are a means of self-expression: their clothes project their personalities. Their clothes are personified by the force of their personalities; Dombey's clothes, on the other hand, depersonify him—not only do they not have life, but they seem to deprive him of life as well. The differences between these two types of clothes is suggested by Carlyle in *Sartor Resartus* when he writes that " 'clothes gave us individuality, distinctions, social polity; clothes have made Men of us; they are threatening to make clothes screens of us.' "[14] The clothes of Cuttle, Toots, and Bunsby give them "individuality" and "distinctions." The clothes of Dombey turn him into a "clothes screen"; they are like the "Church-clothes" that Carlyle discusses that "have become mere hollow Shapes, or Masks, under which no living Figure or Spirit any longer dwells."[15]

Yet Toots's fixation on clothes is still suspicious. Dickens makes a comic allusion to *Sartor Resartus* in the scene in which Toots tries to kiss Susan and is chased out of the house by the dog Diogenes, who tears at his pantaloons:

> Susan screamed, laughed, opened the street-door, and ran down stairs; the bold Toots tumbled staggering out into the street, with Diogenes holding on to one leg of his pantaloons, as if Burgess and Co. were his cooks, and had provided that dainty morsel for his holiday entertainment. (*D&S* 316; ch. 22)

Like Carlyle's Diogenes Teufelsdrockh, Diogenes the dog takes a radical attitude toward clothes in this scene. But why would Dickens show Diogenes tearing into *Toots*'s clothes? Why not Dombey's? After all, Toots is sympathetic, good-hearted, and a member of the community Dickens favors in the conclusion. His clothes seem to give him "individuality" and "distinctions" instead of turning him into a "clothes screen." Is Dickens suggesting through the smooth, solid surface of Cuttle, Bunsby, and Toots that the kind of alternative the Midshipman community offers is also limiting, even suspicious?

Other details strengthen these suspicions. In the last chapter, Toots tells Cuttle and Gills that Susan predicts that Walter may become another Dombey:

> " 'Why . . . under the very eye of Mr. Dombey, there is a foundation going on, upon which a—an Edifice;' that was Mrs. Toots's word," says Mr. Toots exultingly, " 'is gradually rising, perhaps to equal, perhaps excel, that of which he was once the head, and the small beginnings of which (a common fault, but a bad one, Mrs. Toots said) escaped his memory. Thus,' said my wife, 'from his daughter, after all, another Dombey and Son will ascend'—no 'rise;' that was Mrs. Toots's word—'triumphant.' " (D&S 877; ch. 62)

The countercommunity with all of its chaotic, impulsive forces has risen to replace the static, ordered world of Dombey. Dickens has suggested the rich potential in the folly of the Midshipman community; as with the railroad, a productive, lively new world has emerged from the chaos. Yet Dickens questions whether such folly can survive long in a central position, in the position Dombey had inhabited. Another "Edifice" is rising—the word suggests the rigidity and order of Dombey's world, another phallus, not the lively chaos of the Midshipman group. The edifice is even given the same label as the one it is replacing. Along the same lines, the "ungoverned" and wandering Bunsby is finally restrained by Mrs. MacStinger, who hooks him, drags him to the altar, and ties the knot with him. Florence, of course, does not need to be restrained in the conclusion since Dickens has kept her under tight rein throughout the novel. Dickens suggests that once the chaos has produced its positive change, stasis and normalcy set in. What has been the fluid community of fools becomes a set and solid group who are still eccentric but are more restrained and more successful at achieving bourgeois goals. A new wave of chaos must begin the cycle again.

NOTES

1. A similar tendency can be seen in *Martin Chuzzlewit*. As J. Hillis Miller says of this novel, "It is not really even possible to say that the characters are a little mad, for there is no concept of sanity by which they may be

judged . . ." (*Charles Dickens: The World of His Novels* [Cambridge, MA: Harvard Univ. Press, 1965], 88).

2. Quoted in Edgar Johnson, *Charles Dickens: His Tragedy and Triumph*, 2 vols. (New York: Simon and Schuster, 1952), 602.

3. Quoted in ibid., 603.

4. Julian Moynahan, "Dealings with the Firm of Dombey and Son: Firmness versus Wetness," in *Dickens and the Twentieth Century*, ed. John Gross and Gabriel Pearson (Toronto: Univ. of Toronto Press, 1962), 130.

5. John Carey, *The Violent Effigy: A Study of Dickens' Imagination* (London: Faber and Faber, 1973), 101.

6. Kathleen Tillotson, "Dombey and Son," in *Dickens: A Collection of Critical Essays*, ed. Martin Price (Englewood Cliffs, NJ: Prentice-Hall, 1967), 131.

7. Moynahan, "Dealings with the Firm," 126.

8. Jerome Meckier makes a similar point in "Dickens and King Lear: A Myth for Victorian England," *South Atlantic Quarterly* (Winter 1971): 75-90.

9. Michel Foucault, *Madness and Civilization: A History of Insanity in the Age of Reason*, trans. Richard Howard (New York: Pantheon, 1965), x.

10. Moynahan, "Dealings with the Firm," 130, 128.

11. Lyn Pykett, "*Dombey and Son*: A Sentimental Family Romance," *Studies in the Novel* 19 (1987): 19.

12. Sandra Lee Bartky, "Foucault, Femininity, and the Modernization of Patriarchal Power," in *Feminism and Foucault: Reflections on Resistance*, ed. Irene Diamond and Lee Quinby (Boston: Northeastern Univ. Press, 1988), 63-64.

13. Thomas Carlyle, *Sartor Resartus* (New York: Scribner's, n.d.), 52; ch. 10, bk. 1.

14. Ibid., 31; ch. 5, bk. 1.

15. Ibid., 172; ch. 2, bk. 3.

Chapter 8

Little Dorrit's Misfits:
Between the Sun and the Cell

In *Nicholas Nickleby* and *Barnaby Rudge* Dickens attempts to celebrate aberrant characters but ultimately marginalizes them; in *Dombey and Son* he reverses the pattern, at least in part, by celebrating the chaotic energy of foolishness and idiocy, by bringing the marginal to the center. In *Little Dorrit* Dickens continues affirming chaos by showing that only the foolish, idiotic, misfit characters have any chance of escaping the constraints of society and the more physical restraints of prison.[1]

Much attention—some will say too much—has already been focused on the prison imagery in *Little Dorrit*, but most has examined the notion of imprisonment as entrapment or confinement. Less notice has been paid to the idea of surveillance—the opposite extreme of disciplinary restraint.[2] Images of surveillance are prevalent throughout the narrative. The images often suggest Bentham's Panopticon, which revolves around the power of surveillance—a circle of cells at the center of which is an observation tower from which any cell can be seen at any time. Foucault felt that "the perfect disciplinary apparatus" would be one based on the Panopticon: ". . . a single gaze [would] see everything constantly. A central tower would be both the source of light illuminating everything, and a locus of convergence for everything that must be known: a perfect eye that nothing would escape and a centre towards which all gazes would be turned."[3] Ironically, in *Little Dorrit* the literal prisons—the Marshalsea and the Marseilles jail—bear little similarity to the Panopticon; they emphasize confinement more than surveillance. But Dickens portrays a network of Panopticons in this novel, suggesting that surveillance is more diffuse and ubiquitous than a single prison, originating with many different eyes. Society is one such eye, functioning as an unenclosed Panopticon. The eye of Society is central and all-observant because it has been internalized while still functioning as an external force. It is both the "eye" and the "I." It shapes behavior, enforces codes, and nullifies independent will and privacy. The literal prisons, paradoxically, offer an escape from such surveillance.

Foucault describes incarceration and surveillance as the two extreme ends of the discipline spectrum:

> There are two images, then, of discipline. At one extreme, the discipline-blockade, the enclosed institution . . . turned inwards towards negative functions: arresting evil, breaking communications, suspending time. At the other extreme, with panopticism, is the discipline-mechanism: a functional mechanism that must improve the exercise of power by making it lighter, more rapid, more effective; a design of subtle coercion for a society to come. The movement from one project to the other, from a schema of exceptional discipline to one of a generalized surveillance, rests on a historical transformation: the gradual extension of the mechanisms of discipline throughout the seventeenth and eighteenth centuries, their spread throughout the whole social body, the formation of what might be called in general the disciplinary society.[4]

Although Foucault suggests here that society has moved toward "generalized surveillance" and away from the "enclosed institution," certainly the latter is still in effect. In *Little Dorrit* the characters wander between these extreme poles of imprisonment, recapitulating in their experiences the progress of the "mechanisms of discipline" that Foucault describes in the quotation just cited. The Dorrits and Rigaud move from literal prisons to the surveillance of society, while Arthur experiences the process in reverse. But Dickens establishes a small community in *Little Dorrit*, similar to the Midshipman community in *Dombey and Son*, that manages a partial escape from the two poles of discipline through their foolishness, idiocy, and chaotic energies. Through them, Dickens offers some hope of evading prisons.

Dickens uses the sun (and light in general) as an image of surveillance, and contrasts these images with the shadows of prisons. The two images are introduced in chapter 1, book 1, of *Little Dorrit*, entitled "Sun and Shadow." Dickens opens the novel by describing Marseilles "burning in the sun" (*LD* 1). He personifies the sun in this chapter and in the second paragraph connects its inescapable light with the notion of surveillance:

> Everything in Marseilles, and about Marseilles, had stared at the fervid sky, and been stared at in return, until a staring habit had become universal there. Strangers were stared out of countenance by staring white houses, staring white walls, staring white streets, staring tracts of arid road, staring hills from which

verdure was burnt away. . . . Hindoos, Russians, Chinese, Spaniards, Portuguese, Englishmen, Frenchmen, Genoese, Neapolitans, Venetians, Greeks, Turks, descendants from all the builders of Babel, come to trade at Marseilles, sought the shade alike—taking refuge in any hiding place from a sea too intensely blue to be looked at, and a sky of purple, set with one great flaming jewel of fire. (*LD* 1)

The sun stares at everything and causes everything under its power to stare in return. In this description Dickens sets against a chaos of languages—a "Babel" of voices—the one great eye of the sun. He continues opposing chaos and the eye throughout the novel.

In the next paragraph, Dickens describes how those "oppressed by the glare" of the great staring sun try to shut it out with blinds, shutters, and curtains, but all it needs is "a chink or keyhole, and it [shoots] in like a white-hot arrow" (*LD* 2; bk. 1, ch. 1). This image of a "chink" is one Dickens uses recurrently in describing the imprisoned, as I have observed in Chapter 2, but here, although it is again used in conjunction with images of imprisonment, its signification is radically different. In early articles and novels Dickens uses the chink of light as an image of hope for those physically or mentally entrapped. He describes Laura Bridgman, the deaf, dumb, and blind girl at the Perkins Institute, as trapped in "a marble cell . . . with her poor white hand peeping through a chink in the wall, beckoning to some good man for help" (*AN* 32). The chink is the only connection between her locked-up soul and the outside world. Dickens uses the image repeatedly in depictions of more literal prisons. Later in *American Notes* he describes a bleak cell in a New York jail with its one connection to the outside world, its one emblem of hope, being a "high chink in the wall" through which some light could enter (84). The image is used similarly in "A Visit to Newgate" from *Sketches by Boz* (211) and in *A Tale of Two Cities* (37). The Marchioness in *The Old Curiosity Shop* escapes the solitude of her imprisonment by staring through keyholes, which Dickens equates with the chink image in the passage just quoted from *Little Dorrit*. Many of the illustrations of prisoners in *American Notes* and *Barnaby Rudge* portray light shining into a prison cell through a chink in the wall. In all these cases the image offers hope for the imprisoned, a sense that they are not completely isolated, that some escape is possible.

But the image in *Little Dorrit* completely inverts these values. The chink or keyhole here suggests the near impossibility of ever completely escaping surveillance. One can never entirely shut it out. Like prisoners in Bentham's Panopticon, the citizens of Marseilles cannot evade observation. Dickens's inversion of the image suggests that in addition to seeing entrapment in extreme privacy as tragic, he now also sees entrapment in an extreme lack of privacy as equally devastating.

After opening the chapter with images of the oppressive eye, Dickens continues it with a description of another extreme: the dark, close cell. Emphasizing its opposition to surveillance, Dickens describes the Marseilles prison as "so repulsive a place that even the obtrusive stare blinked at it, and left it to such refuse of reflected light as it could find for itself" (LD 2; bk. 1, ch. 1).[5] The cell of Rigaud and John Baptist is described as a tomb that has "no knowledge of the brightness outside" (LD 3; bk. 1, ch. 1). Rigaud's first words curse the sun for not illuminating the cell: " ' To the devil with this Brigand of a Sun that never shines in here!' " (LD 3; bk. 1, ch. 1).[6] The cell, in other words, escapes the torture of the sun, but in its place provides the horrors of confinement. Everything is "deteriorated by confinement" in the cell; everything is burned by the sun outside of it. Images of surveillance and confinement are interwoven not only in this first chapter but throughout the novel.

When Arthur first returns to London and sits in a coffee house preparing himself for visiting his mother, he has a sense of being surveyed by the endless rows of houses around him: "Ten thousand responsible houses surrounded him, frowning . . . heavily on the streets they composed" (LD 28; bk. 1, ch. 3). They weigh down his spirits, reminding him of duty, work, and penitence, particularly as it is Sunday. His mother is a figure of surveillance too, with her judgmental, Old Testament philosophy and her unrelenting sternness. As Arthur walks toward her house, he sees the light in her window, which he says "seems never to have been extinguished since I came home twice a year from school, and dragged my box over this pavement" (LD 31; bk. 1, ch. 3).

Other lights continue the surveillance imagery. In London, even at night, the light in the sky is unrelenting. On his first night back, Arthur looks out from his old bedroom window at "the old red glare in the sky which had seemed to him once upon a time but a nightly reflection of the fiery environment that was presented to his childish fancy in all directions, let it look where it would" (LD 38; bk. 1, ch. 3). The London sky's fierce nighttime stare is even more inescapable than the Marseilles sun because it reminds Arthur of the angry, vindictive tone of his mother and the Old Testament God she proclaims; therefore, the "stare" becomes internalized in a sense of moral codes and guilt. The "eye" becomes the "I."

Society is the ultimate surveillant in this novel; Mr. Dorrit aptly calls it "the Eye of the Great World" (LD 597; bk. 2, ch. 15). Its relentless gaze is abetted by several representatives, chiefly Mrs. Merdle, the Merdles' butler, and Mrs. General. Mrs. Merdle is the universally acknowledged spokesperson for Society, approving or censoring others according to Society's rules of decorum. Others seek out her counsel in determining Society's demands. Fanny plans her life around equaling or perhaps bettering Mrs. Merdle in the eyes of Society. Mrs. Gowan checks with Mrs. Merdle about the propriety of Henry's marriage. Mrs. Merdle personifies Society while enumerating the duties it exacts ("Society really will not have any patience," "Society has made up its mind," [*LD* 391; bk. 1, ch. 33]), making it seem like a god who demands sacrifices. In some ways Mrs. Merdle's Society becomes a version of Mrs. Clennam's God—both are all-seeing, powerful, and vindictive.

If Mrs. Merdle is Society's voice, its eye (or at least one pair of its many eyes) is Merdle's butler. He surveys the guests at the Merdle functions as if passing judgment on them. "He looked on," Dickens tells us, "as few other men could have done" (*LD* 249; bk. 1, ch. 21). His surveillance, as Society's functionary, panics Mr. Merdle, who at all costs tries to avoid his stare and takes himself into custody when confronted by it. Mr. Dorrit is similarly stricken with the butler's stare:

> That stupendous character [the butler] looked at him, in the course of his official looking at the dinners, in a manner that Mr. Dorrit considered questionable. He looked at him, as he passed through the hall and up the staircase, going to dinner, with a glazed fixedness that Mr. Dorrit did not like. Seated at table in the act of drinking, Mr. Dorrit still saw him through his wine-glass, regarding him with a cold and ghostly eye . . . the Chief Butler had him in his supercilious eye, even when that eye was on the plate and other table-garniture; and he never let him out of it. (*LD* 619; bk. 2, ch. 16)

Merdle's and Dorrit's sense of the butler's judgmental nature is not mere paranoia; the butler does judge as he surveys, and his judgment, at least in the case of Merdle, is correct. Unlike the less perceptive throng surrounding Merdle, the butler sees through his sham and knows all along that Merdle is a fake. When the butler is informed that Merdle has killed himself, he evinces no surprise, stating that he always knew Mr. Merdle was no gentleman.

Mrs. General serves as another representative of the great surveillant, Society. Her name, of course, emphasizes her disciplinary function. She makes a living out of knowing Society's dictates, observing her charges, and forming their minds to be in line with what is decorous. She tries to train Fanny and Amy to internalize the eye of Society, to surveil themselves incessantly to make sure they are never pronouncing an independent view, never thinking of anything beyond "prunes and prism." With Amy she attempts to "form a surface" (*LD* 503; bk. 2, ch. 7), but Amy, in typical holy fool fashion, does not take well to surface but instead eschews it and the worldly goods it entails.

Amy, then, does not escape Society's surveillance but does not seem to be very constrained by it either. And although she was born and raised in the Marshalsea, by the end of the novel she has left prisons behind her and is moving away from them. She moves away from one end of the disciplinary spectrum but not into the confines of the other. She is not the only one to effect at least a partial escape; Clennam, Pancks, the Plornishes, Nandy, Maggy, Doyce, and even Flora and Mr. F's aunt also seem to find a middle ground as far from surveillance and cells as possible. Dickens depicts these characters' gravitation toward each other throughout the book. By the end they form a small community in and around Bleeding Heart Yard, one similar to the Wooden Midshipman group that prevails in *Dombey and Son*. Like the Wooden Midshipman community, the Bleeding Heart Yarders are composed of the flotsam and jetsam of society: Amy, the Child of the Marshalsea; Arthur, a Marshalsea debtor; Plornish, a slow and inarticulate ex-Marshalsea inmate; Nandy, a doting old workhouse prisoner; Maggy, the idiot; Doyce, the maverick inventor; Pancks, the frenetic "gypsy" and rebel; Flora, the chronically garrulous widow; and Mr. F's aunt, the senile and severe prophetess.

The name "Bleeding Heart Yard" indicates the community's connection with the foolishness of the sensitive, feeling heart. In the beginning of the novel, the "heart" seems to be weak and broken, but gradually it regroups, rejuvenates, and heals itself, so that it becomes the strong, beating center of the novel. At first only the Plornishes and Doyce are Bleeding Heart Yarders: the Plornishes live there, and Doyce's business is there. But then Arthur joins the community when he becomes Doyce's partner and befriends the Plornishes; Flora and Mr. F's aunt come around to visit Arthur and befriend Amy; Maggy moves in with the Plornishes when the Dorrits leave the Marshalsea; Pancks graduates from being a persecutor of the inhabitants to being a clerk for Doyce and Clennam; and Amy becomes a member as wife of Arthur and friend of all the others. By suggesting that these figures manage a partial escape from surveillance and cells because of their foolishness and idiocy, Dickens adopts a Romantic perspective on mental aberrance, but a perspective that also prefigures Foucault's explorations in this area. It seems Dickens would concur with Foucault's claim that madness in itself has value, that "madness fascinates because it is knowledge."[7] This knowledge "so inaccessible, so formidable, the Fool, in his innocent idiocy, already possesses."[8]

Dickens values foolishness in *Little Dorrit* partly by using elements of the holy fool tradition in his depiction of Amy. Traditionally, as we have seen in Chapter 3, holy fools have physical abnormalities; often they are dwarfs or partly lame. Amy, of course, is freakishly small, with the body of a child but the face of a grown woman. Like Smike, Barnaby, Toots, and Cuttle before her, and like Jenny Wren and Sloppy after her, Amy physically combines the child and the adult, an image that suggests, in typical holy fool fashion, that she has carried into maturity some of the innocence of youth. When Arthur first looks closely at her, he finds

> that her diminutive figure, small features, and slight spare dress, gave her the appearance of being much younger than she was. A woman, probably of not less than two-and-twenty, she might have been passed in the street for little more than half that age. Not that her face was very youthful, for in truth there was more consideration and care in it than naturally belonged to her utmost years; but she was so little and light, so noiseless and shy, and appeared so conscious of being out of place among the three hard elders, that she had all the manner and much of the appearance of a subdued child. (*LD* 52; ch. 5)

Amy also wears the "slight spare" clothes that associate Dickens's other holy fools with a disregard for surface and with a tendency to see beyond surface. Her clothes are not just a sign of her poverty, for she chooses to keep them after her family comes into its fortune, and she resumes wearing her thin dress when she tends Arthur in the Marshalsea. She sees her clothes as signs of her identity, and as such, she insists upon them. Naturally her attitude appears like foolishness to her worldly family. Fanny calls her a "little Fool," with more accuracy than she intends (*LD* 243; ch. 20). Dickens's use of holy fool images affirms not only Amy's way of life but foolishness in general by recalling a tradition in which foolishness was valued as a kind of knowledge and as a means of countering authority.

With Amy, Dickens finally portrays a female fool-protagonist with a physical abnormality. Dickens depicts earlier female protagonists, even those with the behavioral and spiritual traits of holy fools, as perfect specimens of femininity and beauty.[9] But Amy is not as confined by norms of beauty as is Florence in *Dombey and Son* or Little Nell in *The Old Curiosity Shop*, nor can her abnormality be normalized, as are the Marchioness's manner and Mrs. Nickleby's speech. Amy's diminutive stature is permanent and indeed freakish. Yet it is significant that Dickens chooses to make her a freak of *littleness* as opposed to largeness or some other, more grotesque abnormality like Smike's or Sloppy's ricket-ridden frames. Amy's smallness accentuates her femininity by allowing her to be unobtrusive and "noiseless" (*LD* 52; bk. 1, ch. 5). Ultra-docile, Amy outnorms the norms of behavior for Victorian women. She is the Angel in the House done one better by being so small she takes up less space, intrudes less, makes less noise. So while Dickens tries to

free Amy from the limited range he has given to other female fool-protago-
nists, free her from norms of appearance while still making her attractive, he
ultimately confines her, at the same time, to an even more rigid code of
femininity. He still cannot picture an unattractive, unfeminine fool as a
female protagonist.

Amy's freakish smallness can be partially explained by her refusal of food,
another trait that emphasizes her femininity. In order to feed her father, she
saves the food that Mrs. Clennam gives her (LD 81; bk. 1, ch. 8), and she
refuses the food Arthur offers her, suggesting that Maggy might take it
instead (LD 170-71; bk. 1, ch. 14). This behavior bears similarities to that of
anorexics. Susan Bordo writes that the anorexic's main goal is "to kill of the
body's spontaneities entirely. That is: to cease to experience . . . hungers and
desires."[10] Amy seems to be driven by such a goal, not just in her suppression
of hunger but also in her repression of her desire for Arthur. In mythologizing
her love for Arthur in a fairy tale she tells to Maggy, Amy tries to kill off her
love for Arthur into art. Through the story, Amy tries to convince herself of
the impossibility of fulfilling her desire, envisioning for herself a lonely,
sexless life. Clearly, for Amy hungers are not meant to be fulfilled. Bordo
argues that psychopathologies like anorexia nervosa are not "anomalies or
aberrations . . . but characteristic expressions of a culture."[11] Amy's desire to
kill off her hungers is the effect of a culture that has taught her to believe
that women are designed to meet the desires of others, not to fulfill their
own, to serve without being seen or heard. In Amy's world, large, noisy
women like Flora are laughable or pathetic, models of what should be avoided
in female behavior at all costs. Bordo calls anorexia nervosa the "crystallization of culture," and certainly Amy is the crystallization of her culture's
expectations of women—a compact package of docility, devotion, and duty.
Her body is one prison Amy cannot entirely escape; it has been constructed
by her culture and, more important, so has her *sense* of self. To maintain a
positive sense of who she is, she must continue being small, quiet, selfless.
Sandra Bartky suggests that "a panoptical male connoisseur resides within
the consciousness of most women";[12] it is that surveillant whose approval
must be won. Such an internal surveillant and such a personal prison make
escape difficult. Amy does manage a partial escape, however, in finally
allowing herself to fulfill her sexual desire for Arthur.

Amy's foolishness, then, offers her a partial escape from society's dictates
because by not caring about fashion, fortune, and high society, she evades
some of the effects of its surveillance. Yet she is still trapped in a body and
a sense of feminine behavior that her culture has constructed. This prison
she must continue to carry with her.

Maggy, Amy's idiot tag-along, also manages a partial escape through her foolishness. Although she is neither a holy nor a wise fool, Dickens uses many of the images in describing her that he used for earlier holy and wise fools. For instance, she has the fool's customary tattered garments (much more worn and absurd than Amy's), physical deformities, and the combination of youth and age (she thinks she is ten years old even though she is an adult):

> She was about eight-and-twenty, with large bones, large features, large feet and hands, large eyes and no hair. Her large eyes were limpid and almost colourless; they seemed to be very little affected by light, and to stand unnaturally still. There was also that attentive listening expression in her face which is seen in the faces of the blind; but she was not blind, having one tolerably serviceable eye. . . .A great white cap, with a quantity of opaque frilling that was always flapping about, apologised for Maggy's baldness. . . .A commission of haberdashers could alone have reported what the rest of her poor dress was made of; but it had a strong general resemblance to seaweed, with here and there a gigantic tea-leaf. Her shawl looked particularly like a tea-leaf, after long infusion. (*LD* 101; ch. 9, bk. 1)

The tattered garments here suggest a disregard for surface but do not underscore a visionary nature, a tendency to see beyond surface, as they do with other fools. Maggy has no prophetic or mystical visions. In fact, her vision is limited. Other Dickens fools have abnormal eyes, but usually their defects indicate a heightened vision. Newman Noggs's and Bunsby's two-directional eyes and Barnaby's and Mr. Dick's protruding eyes suggest that their vision is somehow superior, expanded. But Maggy has only one "serviceable" eye, and both are colorless and lifeless. She has none of the snappy retorts of wise fools, nor is she unusually self-sacrificing and good-hearted as are holy fools. On the contrary, she is rather selfish, caring for her own needs over Amy's, and whining when they have to spend the night outside the Marshalsea. In short, she has no redeeming factors to compensate for her idiocy. Dickens insists that she be accepted on her own terms: clumsy, idiotic, childish, ugly—and unfeminine—the kind of grotesque he could not allow his female protagonists to be.

Dickens's uncompromising portrayal of Maggy bears a resemblance to Wordsworth's mendicant in "The Old Cumberland Beggar," who wanders the countryside and begs for food. Wordsworth does not develop him as a great icon of romantic values, meditating on nature's wonders and communing with the wildlife. In fact, the beggar seems to notice nature very little, if at all, and actively tries to keep birds away from his food. He does serve a useful function, Wordsworth asserts, by reminding the villagers of their own good fortune, but this is the only practical justification Wordsworth gives him. As Cleanth Brooks has suggested, Wordsworth's presentation of the beggar is radical and challenging;[13] Dickens's characterization of Maggy is equally so. According to Brooks, Wordsworth's argument is: "They also serve who only creep and beg." The poem, Brooks asserts, is

> a plea that some noble animal may enjoy its right to continue its natural freedom and to live out its life in its own accustomed way. The beggar ought, for example, to have around him the pleasant song of the birds, whether he can hear it or whether he cares to hear it. He ought to be allowed to behold "the countenance of the horizontal sun," even if his eyes have now "Been doomed so long to settle upon earth."[14]

Similarly, by making Maggy an integral part of the countercommunity and keeping her there, keeping her foolish and even annoying, Dickens suggests that Maggy is worthwhile, even as a mess, a chaotic creature who seems to have nothing practical or even impractical to offer. Dickens advocates, through her, foolishness for its own sake.

Maggy's idiocy makes her oblivious to society and therefore enables her partially to escape the effects of surveillance, but she is drawn to the other extreme, the safe confines of prison. The Marshalsea is home to her, and her idea of heaven is a hospital, another prison-type institution, since she once stayed in one and was given decent food and affection. But Maggy eventually escapes prisons as well as surveillance by being incorporated into the Bleeding Heart Yard community where she has safety and comfort without confinement. And unlike Amy, Maggy is not trapped in the prison of femininity. Maggy does not care about being docile or dainty and quite eagerly satisfies her healthy appetite whenever she can. In fact, ensuring her own creature comforts seems to be Maggy's main focus in life. Her idiocy renders her unsusceptible to the disciplinary practices that confine Amy.

With the Plornishes, Dickens again shows how foolishness facilitates some escape from surveillance and confinement through nonsensical play. The little store they set up with the help of Dorrit seems one of the few truly charmed spots in all of London—an oasis in a bleak metropolis. They establish this oasis by playing house. In the parlor of their shop they paint the exterior of a thatched cottage on one of the walls. They call it Happy Cottage, and the paint in conjunction with their imaginations transform the parlor into a pastoral retreat:

> No Poetry and no Art ever charmed the imagination more than the union of the two in this counterfeit cottage charmed Mrs. Plornish. It was nothing to her that Plornish had a habit of leaning against it as he smoked his pipe after work . . .

when his back swallowed up the dwelling, when his hands in his pockets
uprooted the blooming garden and laid waste the adjacent country. To Mrs.
Plornish, it was still a most beautiful cottage, a most wonderful deception . . . To
come out into the shop after it was shut, and hear her father sing a song inside
this cottage, was a perfect Pastoral to Mrs. Plornish, the Golden Age revived.
(*LD* 574; bk. 2, ch. 13)

Happy Cottage is not just a retreat for the Plornishes, but for others who
drop in as well, such as Pancks and John Baptist. It creates a sense of home,
community, and peacefulness hard to come by in the impoverished world of
the Bleeding Heart Yard inhabitants. Yet it is patently absurd. The perspective of the cottage is comically distorted, and the effect of it depends entirely
on one's capacity for self-deception, for playing. But Dickens affirms these
qualities as being not only positive but essential for eluding surveillance and
prisons, for creating a life worth living.[15]

Dickens indicates that the Bleeding Heart Yard inhabitants, in general,
engage in play, romanticizing their neighborhood much as the Plornishes
transform their shop into Happy Cottage. The inhabitants invent numerous
fanciful stories to explain how the area acquired the name "Bleeding Heart
Yard." Tales of murder and broken hearts predominate in their explanations.
The Yarders are united in denying the reports of "antiquaries who delivered
learned lectures in the neighbourhood, showing the Bleeding Heart to have
been the heraldic cognizance of the old family to whom the property had
once belonged" (*LD* 136; bk. 1, ch. 12). Dickens, along with the Bleeding
Heart Yarders, prefers the fanciful to the factual. With lives defined by work
and poverty, "the Bleeding Heart Yarders had reason enough for objecting
to be despoiled of the one little golden grain of poetry that sparkled in it"
(*LD* 136).

Pancks too indulges his fancy by playing the gypsy fortune-teller, reading
palms, hinting at secrets, making prophecies, and generally astounding Amy.
Pancks is the epitome of chaotic energy with his puffing, snorting, and blowing
and his darting in and out of scenes. Dickens allies him with the chaotic energy
of the railroad in *Dombey* by referring to Pancks as a "steam-engine" (although
Pancks's engine is of the tugboat and barge variety) (*LD* 148; ch. 13, bk. 1).
Pancks functions as a wise fool—a comic, clever, spry figure who ultimately
plays his most important role in undermining the authority of Casby through a
slapstick but highly symbolic attack on the old man. Long a slave of Casby, who
pressures him to incessantly "squeeze" the Bleeding Heart Yarders for money,
Pancks finally declares his independence in the conclusion of the novel by
proclaiming Casby's hypocrisy to the assembled crowd in Bleeding Heart Yard,

knocking off Casby's hat, trimming its rim, and cutting his flowing locks. This eccentric act of rebellion liberates Pancks and frees the Bleeding Heart Yarders as well, for it topples the image of a benign, superior being that Casby had set up for himself in order to control them. Dickens demonstrates through Pancks that chaotic energy is superior, finally, to the staid power of respectable Casbys and that it is a potent liberating force.

Doyce's creative energy, although not as poetic as the Plornish's or as frenetic as Pancks's, helps him achieve independence with his business and success abroad, if not at home, with his inventions. Like Arthur, Amy, Pancks, and the Plornishes, Doyce does not much care to win Society's approval, so he is not very inhibited by its surveillance. He pursues his own inventions and utilizes them even if no one else takes advantage of them. His success enables Arthur and Pancks to gain some independence too, for he creates a working environment for both of them in which they can thrive. Doyce is treated by the Barnacles, the family that is metonymic for Society, as a "public offender" because he has dared to have an original invention for which he hoped to obtain a patent. The Barnacles and even Meagles consider him " 'a man not quite able to take care of himself' " (*LD* 190), because his creative thinking separates him from the mainstream of society: "[Meagles's] curious sense of a general superiority to Daniel Doyce . . . [was] founded, not so much on anything in Doyce's personal character, as on the mere fact of his being an originator and a man out of the beaten track of other men . . . " (*LD* 194; bk. 1, ch. 16). Because he is "out of the beaten track of other men," Doyce manages to sidestep the surveillance and prisons that belong to that track.

Dickens shows Flora's foolishness to be both liberating and confining. She is chiefly imprisoned in herself—in her delusions of a romance between herself and Arthur Clennam and in her nonsensical, garrulous monologues. She alienates Arthur with her silly flirtations. Yet her loquacity allows her to create an illusion not unlike that of the Plornishes. She plays out her monologues like little dramas, and they establish her (if only in her own eyes and only part of the time) as still young, attractive, flirtatious, and vivacious.[16] They liberate her from the confines of her dull existence in her father's home, from the confines of reality, just as the Plornish's Happy Cottage allows for an escape from the quotidian. By the end of the narrative, Flora evolves away from the most limiting aspects of her personality through her sincere over-tures of friendship to Amy and in her enjoyment of Amy and Arthur's wedding. Although Flora tells Amy that she will "retire into privacy" now that Amy and Clennam are getting married, she does not display "the least signs of seclusion about her" at the wedding and in fact is "wonderfully smart, and [enjoys] the ceremonies mightily, though in a fluttered way" (*LD* 825-26; bk. 2, ch. 34). She has risen above her own disappointments and can take pleasure in the happiness of others, even in the happiness of her rival for Arthur's affections. She is still garrulous, but she is not as bound up in herself. Her monologues have opened into dialogues (which she still dominates due to her loquacity), and one feels her garrulousness will not be such a liability in the community of oddity in Bleeding Heart Yard.[17]

The absurdity of Flora's loquaciousness is counterpointed by the brief, nonsensical pronouncements of Mr. F's aunt, a kind of comic Teiresias, who seems so far outside the realm of rational discourse that it is difficult to imagine her entrapped in the disciplinary structures of society:

> The major characteristics discoverable by the stranger in Mr. F's Aunt, were extreme severity and grim taciturnity; sometimes interrupted by a propensity to offer remarks in a deep warning voice, which, being totally uncalled for by anything said by anybody, and traceable to no association of ideas, confounded and terrified the mind. Mr. F's Aunt may have thrown in these observations on some system of her own, and it may have been ingenious, or even subtle; but the key to it was wanted. (*LD* 157; ch. 13, bk. 1)

Although one of her proclamations is " 'I hate a fool!' " she is one herself, being a nonsensical and "all-licensed" critic, whose complete absurdity allows her to say whatever she likes. She is yet another character with whom Dickens suggests the power of nonsense. Flora, who is always silly and bubbly in her monologues, needs Mr. F's aunt as an alter ego, for the old lady uses her proclamations to vent some spleen, something Flora never does or never is able to do.[18] While Flora is being gracious about Amy and Arthur's marriage, Mr. F's aunt vents hostility by pronouncing, in reference to Arthur, " 'Bring him for'ard, and I'll chuck him out o' winder!' " (*LD* 820; bk. 2, ch. 34). Dickens shows that Flora understands the importance of nonsense by indicating how she values Mr. F's aunt. Flora describes her, quite seriously, as a "legacy," and she tolerates her exceedingly difficult tempers with perfect equanimity (*LD* 159; bk. 1, ch. 13). In fact, Dickens describes Flora as being "proud" of the peculiarities of Mr. F's aunt (*LD* 159).

Dickens celebrates even Arthur, staid as he is, for his foolishness. In typical holy fool fashion, Arthur disregards worldly goods and social pressures: he leaves a stable position with his mother's company; he does not yield to the pressure Mrs. Gowan exerts to make him corroborate her opinion of Pet Meagles; in spite of his mother's strong protests, he perseveres in exploring his suspicions about his family's wrongdoing, even though the answers he finds may hurt him financially; and he takes the full blame for the ruin of Doyce's company even when warned about Society's harsh judgment on him. Such disregard for money and for societal approval places him on the margins of the disciplining influence of Society's surveillance. He has a strong inner sense of what is right, and he follows it with no regard to Society's dictates. He also has no desire to be greatly wealthy, so he is free of the pressure to compete for worldly goods. Of course, these qualities do not keep him out of debtor's prison, but the ties he has formed with Pancks, Cavaletto, Meagles, Amy, and Doyce ensure his escape from the Marshalsea.

Because of their chaotic, creative energies, their idiocy, and their disregard for or obliviousness to Society's dictates, the Bleeding Heart Yarders achieve more freedom than any other characters in the novel. Mrs. Merdle may still have an honored social place at the conclusion of the novel, but she is a slave to Society as is Fanny, Mrs. Gowan, Mrs. General, the Barnacle crew, and most others.[19] Even the Meagles toady to Society's demands too devotedly to gain much independence. It is significant that Dickens chooses not to include them in the final, happy resolution tableau at the wedding. By celebrating the misfits of Bleeding Heart Yard, Dickens suggests the potential inherent in the marginal, in what is thrown out or disregarded by the mainstream of society, in rubbish. The Bleeding Heart Yard misfits, with all their tattered clothes, their garbled idiolects, their nonsensical actions, and their decayed environs, are trash in a utilitarian world, yet Dickens upholds them, as he does the dust heaps and misfits in *Our Mutual Friend*, as sources of a hidden wealth.

The titles of the closing chapters—"Closing In," "Closed," "Going," "Going," and "Gone,"—emphasize the movement of the novel from confinement and surveillance to escape. "Closing In" and "Closed" narrate a series of experiences of entrapment and surveillance—Mrs. Clennam trapped by blackmail and surveilled by Rigaud and by people in the streets as she heads to the Marshalsea, and Rigaud trapped by the collapsed house. But the last three chapters, "Going," "Going," and "Gone," suggest an escape from confinement and surveillance. These chapters narrate Panck's rebellion, Tattycoram's departure from Miss Wade, Arthur's release from the Marshalsea, and Amy and Arthur's marriage, all of which suggest escape from prisons or an assertion of free will that defies surveillance.

Some readers have suggested that the repetition of the word "down" in the final two paragraphs of the novel makes the conclusion negative. Amy and Clennam go "down into a modest life . . . down to give a mother's care . . . to Fanny's neglected children . . . down to give a tender nurse and friend to Tip . . ." (*LD* 826; bk. 2, ch. 34). Certainly the conclusion is restrained.

But although "down" often connotes failure, death, or regression, there is no reason that it must have a negative value in this passage. In fact, considering that Merdle's and Dorrit's plans are built "up"—Dorrit builds castles in the air, and Merdle's plans "[go] on and [go] up" (*LD* 570; bk. 2, ch. 12)—down seems a preferable direction. If one goes down, one may escape surveillance. Even Bleeding Heart Yard is down: "the ground had so risen about Bleeding Heart Yard that you got into it down a flight of steps" (*LD* 135; bk. 1, ch. 12). In a novel where light images are often negative because of their connection to surveillance, it is not surprising to see the usual connotations of "down" inverted too.

In the final paragraphs, Amy and Clennam head away from the prison and into their new lives. The narrator tells us that they walk out into the sun, but it is not the torturous sun of Marseilles; it is a muted sun—an "autumn morning" sun, although still bright (*LD* 826; bk. 2, ch. 34). They pass through their lives, we are told, "in sunshine and in shade" (*LD* 826; bk. 2, ch. 34). Since sunshine and light in general have stood for surveillance and shade for escape from surveillance but also for prisons, the phrase suggests a partial escape from the two poles of discipline that have been presented throughout the novel and that Foucault analyzes in *Discipline and Punish*.

The Bleeding Heart Yard misfits' success in achieving some freedom and independence is foreshadowed by an odd image in the preface to *Little Dorrit*, an image that harks back to *Dombey and Son*. In the preface, Dickens describes visiting the old site of the Marshalsea jail and encountering "the smallest boy [he] ever conversed with, carrying the largest baby [he] ever saw" (*LD* xvii). The image is strikingly similar to the figure of the dwarf child carrying a giant baby that Dickens places at the center of *Dombey and Son*. In *Dombey and Son* the odd pair is thrown out of the church on the morning of Dombey's wedding; they represent all the aberrant types who have been marginalized by Dombey and his sphere, but particularly Florence and the grown "babies" who surround her (*D&S* 439; ch. 31). But the figures Dickens describes encountering by Marshalsea Place are not being victimized; they seem to be perfectly at home and in control, particularly the boy, who strikes Dickens as "supernaturally intelligent" (*LD* xvii). He relates to Dickens a narrative of the place and its prison. The author, in essence, is being guided by the disproportionate pair. The tableau is memorable: Dickens, the author who was never able freely to articulate his own experiences of imprisonment, being told the history of the Marshalsea by two freakish figures.[20]

The image is an apt preface for *Little Dorrit*, for in this novel misfit characters do seem to be more in control of their lives than the more traditionally normal types like the Meagles, Mrs. Merdle, the Gowans, and

Dorrit, whose attempts to fit in to the fashionable world enslave him more than the Marshalsea ever did. In this novel, Dickens depicts the "spread" of the "disciplinary society," a society of surveillance and cells,[21] but he finds promise in the kind of figures who seem most pathetic in his earlier works— idiots, fools, misfits. For to be misfit in this novel is to *not fit* into the prisons of society, to be unaffected by surveillance; to be misfit is to escape.

Perhaps Dickens saw in the image of the unusually small, intelligent boy carrying the unusually large baby something that reminded him of himself as a boy, wandering around the Marshalsea, saddled with responsibilities too large for him. Perhaps he also saw the boy as an appropriate image for himself even as an adult, for part of his psyche was still trapped in that childhood experience and part of him always felt overburdened with his cares. But the scene is also emblematic of an aspect of Dickens's creative process. His being told a tale of imprisonment by a freakish figure suggests that aberrant characters in general reveal their narratives to him, verbally or sometimes nonverbally through their physical appearances and situations. But somehow they speak to him—they signify—and to the rest of the world he articulates their tales.

NOTES

1. Dickens may have identified more with these figures during the writing of *Little Dorrit* than at any previous time. As Edgar Johnson points out, while beginning *Little Dorrit* Dickens wrote to Leigh Hunt that he was feeling " 'as infirm of purpose as Macbeth, as errant as Mad Tom, and as ragged as Timon.' " Johnson suggests that imprisonment was an even more potent subject for Dickens at this time because he felt he was trapped in his marriage (*Charles Dickens: His Tragedy and Triumph*, vol. 2 [New York: Simon and Schuster, 1952], 838, 885).

2. Michael Greenstein briefly examines images of staring in "Liminality in *Little Dorrit*" (*Dickens Quarterly* 7, no. 2 [1990]: 275-283).

3. Michel Foucault, *Discipline and Punish: The Birth of the Prison*, trans. Alan Sheridan (New York: Pantheon, 1977), 173.

4. Ibid., 209.

5. Although the cell is free of the intrusive and glaring sun that tortures the rest of Marseilles, it is not entirely free of surveillance. The cell has a "grating of iron bars . . . by means of which it could be always inspected from the gloomy staircase on which the grating gave" (*LD* 2).

6. In spite of the insistent descriptions of the prison's gloom, Phiz's illustration of the scene depicts light pouring in the window of Rigaud and Cavaletto's cell.

7. Michel Foucault, *Madness and Civilization: A History of Insanity in the Age of Reason*, trans. Richard Howard (New York: Pantheon, 1965), 21.

8. Ibid., 21-22.

9. He flirts with making Esther an unattractive protagonist in *Bleak House*, but of course he restores her beauty in the conclusion.

10. Susan Bordo, "Anorexia Nervosa: Psychopathology as the Crystallization of Culture," in *Feminism and Foucault: Reflections on Resistance*, ed. Irene Diamond and Lee Quinby (Boston: Northeastern Univ. Press, 1988), 93.

11. Ibid., 89.

12. Sandra Lee Bartky, "Foucault, Femininity, and the Modernization of Patriarchal Power," in *Feminism and Foucault: Reflections on Resistance*, ed. Irene Diamond and Lee Quinby (Boston: Northeastern Univ. Press, 1988), 72.

13. Cleanth Brooks, "Wordsworth and Human Suffering: Notes on Two Early Poems," in *Sensibility to Romanticism: Essays Presented to Frederick A. Pottle*, ed. Frederick W. Hilles and Harold Bloom (New York: Oxford Univ. Press, 1965), 379.

14. Ibid., 379.

15. The art that the Plornishes have created with the cottage is not great art by any connoisseur's requisites for the term, but it is art honestly and enthusiastically enjoyed. Likewise, Nandy's singing would not be likely to please music critics. "Society" would no doubt pronounce both distasteful, but the Plornishes are indifferent to society's judgments. As Michael Cotsell has pointed out, "Dickens . . . characteristically associates the assumption of connoisseurship with mental slavishness" ("Politics and Peeling Frescoes: Layard of Ninevah and *Little Dorrit*," *Dickens Studies Annual* 15 [1986]: 184), as is clear in the characterizations of Meagles, Dorrit and Gowan:

    > Meagles's vanity and lack of judgment in regard to art, and his willingness to be imposed upon, are symptomatic of something in him that operates in other areas of his life, conspicuously in his relations with the Barnacles and Stiltstalkings. The assumption of connoisseurship in the Dorrit family, the willingness to be taken about Italy by Mrs. General, are signs of Dorrit's slavishness. The species of modern British artist represented by Henry Gowan thrives on this willingness to be imposed upon. (Cotsell, "Politics," 185)

    The Plornishes are free of such slavishness. Good art to them is whatever pleases them, whatever helps to transform their world.

16. See Nancy Metz, "The Blighted Tree and the Book of Fate: Female Models of Storytelling in *Little Dorrit*," *Dickens Studies Annual* 18 (1989): 231.

17. Like Maggy, Flora freely fulfills her appetites, allowing herself to be guided more by them than by the norms of appearance and behavior for women. But unlike Maggy, Flora is still conscious of these norms and

therefore is troubled by her obesity and feels compelled to hide her drinking.

18. Metz, "The Blighted Tree," 231; Elaine Showalter, "Guilt, Authority, and the Shadows of *Little Dorrit*," *Nineteenth-Century Fiction* 34 (1979): 36-39.

19. Mr. Merdle escapes society's surveillance through suicide, a choice that does not seem at all insane but in fact quite rational in the context of the novel. As Barbara Gates writes in *Victorian Suicide* (Princeton, NJ: Princeton Univ. Press, 1988), "far from being immoral or the act of a lunatic, after mid-century, suicide could seem a very sane retreat for the down-and-out Victorian Briton" (60). Dickens reflects this changing attitude in his depiction of Merdle.

20. Just as the figure in *Dombey* of the small child and the giant baby could be read as Florence and her father (or Toots or Cuttle), so can the tiny child and giant baby in the preface to *Little Dorrit* be seen as Amy and her father, the child taking care of a large, burdensome baby.

21. Foucault, *Discipline*, 209.

Chapter 9

Conclusion: The Voiceless Voiced, the Imprisoned Set Free

Dickens's early childhood experiences of imprisonment and isolation led him throughout his life to focus on prisoners of private worlds and private languages. His personal interest paralleled a general public interest in such figures as asylum and prison reforms raised questions about the place of the aberrant in society. Dickens's personal fascination and his concerns for social reform intertwine in his many characterizations of idiots, madmen, and other prisoners. Inhabitants of private worlds become the structural and thematic—and often incoherent, nonsensical, and ragged—focuses of many of his novels. Through them he voices a distrust of institutionalization and normalization, advocating a greater openness to aberrancy, chaos, and irrationality. Through them he also suggests that often incoherence, nonsense, and fragmented visions and speech offer a more valid and trustworthy perspective on the world than sophisticated rhetoric and logical constructions.

Yet Dickens is not consistent in his approach to these characters. He became increasingly conservative in his attitude toward prisoners as he got older, as can be seen in his magazine articles, while at the same time he became more sympathetic to imprisoned characters in his fiction. In early novels, such as *Nicholas Nickleby* and *Barnaby Rudge*, he attempted to bring idiot characters like Smike and Barnaby to the center of the novels but ended up marginalizing them in the text. In later novels, such as *Dombey and Son*, *Little Dorrit*, and *Our Mutual Friend*, he brings the aberrant to the center and keeps them there, although with some qualifications. His struggle to incorporate the imprisoned types suggests that in spite of his humanitarian attitudes, part of him was deeply troubled by them and wished to segregate, even silence them. His attitude toward his female fools is particularly ambivalent. He seems not to recognize the peculiar prisons Victorian women suffered, and, in fact, he plays the jailer to female characters whom he constrains, subdues, and normalizes: the quieted Mrs. Nickleby, the refined Marchioness, the ever-proper Florence and ever-docile Amy, to name a few. He could never wholeheartedly celebrate aberrancy in women, although with more minor characters, such as Maggy in *Little Dorrit* and Jenny Wren in *Our Mutual Friend*, he makes his greatest strides in this direction. Dickens's failure to incorporate and fully celebrate his early aberrant characters, male and female, is at least as interesting as his success in later novels, for it reveals just how difficult it is actually to carry through with liberal notions about the idiot, the madman, and the prisoner.

Throughout his career, Dickens's characterizations of these figures demonstrates his awareness and suspicion of the increasing trend toward institutionalization and normalization of the aberrant. Prefiguring Foucault in his questioning of this trend, Dickens at times recapitulates the history of the treatment of the insane and prisoners in the histories of his characters, thereby suggesting the danger in the increase of "mechanisms of discipline" in society.[1] In the last half of his career, Dickens affirms aberrancy most strongly, clearly showing that idiots, madmen, and prisoners often lack the compensatory gifts he gives to his early imprisoned characters and that they must be accepted on their own terms, valueless by utilitarian standards.

In *Little Dorrit*, the first of the last four great novels of his career, Dickens finally dissolves the barriers between the unimprisoned and the imprisoned by showing that everyone is a prisoner and that the "mechanisms of discipline" that extend the prison walls throughout society are not simply negative, for they are responsible for the construction of identity, of personhood; they do not simply destroy or exclude—they create.[2] Amy's selflessness and devotion, predominantly positive traits except when they threaten to deny her a life of her own, are created through such disciplinary mechanisms. Yet the degree of imprisonment is not the same for everyone; Dickens suggests that imprisonment and surveillance can be moderated, and he shows this through a community made up of several ex-Marshalsea prisoners, a former workhouse inmate, and several idiots. These characters manage an escape from confinement and surveillance specifically because they are misfits in society. Dickens's portrayal of aberrant characters has evolved radically by the time he writes this novel. From sympathizing with them as the isolated and marginalized figures trapped in extreme privacy, characters who should be more openly incorporated in society, he comes to see them as the only ones who manage to circumvent, to a degree, society's many prisons. In *Little Dorrit*, Dickens shows these characters forming a small community in which they can escape isolation and also escape the trap of "fitting" in society. In the final analysis then, Dickens came to see aberrancy, privacy, and rebellion as necessary to any kind of worthwhile, independent life. Private worlds and private languages, when they do not completely isolate, provide alternatives to a nullifying, mainstream existence.

Dickens's insistence upon figures trapped in private worlds and private languages indicates that their plight is fundamentally connected to his concept of his role as an author. Distrustful of authorities—from his own parents to religious and political leaders, particularly members of Parliament—he hesitates to claim his own authority as an author; he partially circumvents the problem by using his role as author to give voice to those who have no voice or whose voices have been ignored. In pronouncing what should be the role of members of Parliament, Carlyle, in *Chartism*, hits upon a phrase that perhaps best summarizes what Dickens strives to do throughout his characterizations of idiots, madmen, and other prisoners—"interpret and articulate the dumb deep want of the people!"[3]

NOTES

1. Michel Foucault, *Discipline and Punish: The Birth of the Prison*, trans. Alan Sheridan (*New York: Pantheon*, 1977), 209.
2. Ibid., 209; Michael G. Mahon, *Foucault's Nietzschean Genealogy: A Study of Michel Foucault's Nietzschean Problematic, 1961-1975* (Albany: SUNY Press, 1992), 288.
3. Thomas Carlyle, *Chartism, Critical and Miscellaneous Essays*, vol. 4 (New York: AMS Press, 1969), 121.

BIBLIOGRAPHY

PRIMARY SOURCES

Major Works by Dickens

American Notes and Pictures from Italy. New York: Oxford Univ. Press, 1987.

Barnaby Rudge. New York: Oxford Univ. Press, 1987.

Bleak House. New York: Oxford Univ. Press, 1987.

Christmas Books. New York: Oxford Univ. Press, 1987.

Christmas Stories. New York: Oxford Univ. Press, 1987.

David Copperfield. New York: Oxford Univ. Press, 1987.

Dombey and Son. New York: Oxford Univ. Press, 1987.

Great Expectations. New York: Oxford Univ. Press, 1987.

Hard Times. New York: Oxford Univ. Press, 1987.

The Letters of Charles Dickens. The Pilgrim Ed. Vols. 1-6. Oxford: Clarendon Press, 1965-1988.

Little Dorrit. New York: Oxford Univ. Press, 1987.

Martin Chuzzlewit. New York: Oxford Univ. Press, 1987.

The Mystery of Edwin Drood. New York: Oxford Univ. Press, 1987.

Nicholas Nickleby. New York: Oxford Univ. Press, 1987.

The Old Curiosity Shop. New York: Oxford Univ. Press, 1987.

Oliver Twist. New York: Oxford Univ. Press, 1987.

Our Mutual Friend. New York: Oxford Univ. Press, 1987.

The Pickwick Papers. New York: Oxford Univ. Press, 1987.

Sketches by Boz. New York: Oxford Univ. Press, 1987.

A Tale of Two Cities. New York: Oxford Univ. Press, 1987.

The Uncommercial Traveller and Reprinted Pieces. New York: Oxford Univ. Press, 1987.

Articles by Dickens

"A Curious Dance Round a Curious Tree." *Household Words*. No. 95. 17 Jan. 1852: 385-89.

"The Demeanor of Murderers." *Household Words*. No. 325. 14 June 1856: 505-7.

"The Finishing Schoolmaster." *Household Words*. No. 60. 17 May 1851: 169-71.

"Nurse's Stories." *The Uncommercial Traveller and Reprinted Pieces*. Oxford: Oxford Univ. Press, 1987.

"Pet Prisoners." *Household Words*. No. 5. 27 Apr. 1850: 97-103.

"Preliminary Word." *Household Words*. No. 1. 30 Mar. 1850: 1.

"The Restoration of Shakespeare's *Lear* to the Stage." *The Examiner* 4 Feb. 1838: 77-81.

"Supposing." *Household Words*. No. 76. 6 Sept. 1851: 576.

"A Visit to Newgate." *Sketches by Boz*. Oxford: Oxford Univ. Press, 1987.

"A Walk in the Workhouse." *Household Words*. No. 9. 25 May 1850: 204-7.

"A Wapping Workhouse." *The Uncommercial Traveller and Reprinted Pieces*. New York: Oxford Univ. Press, 1987.

Articles by Dickens and Others

Dickens, Charles, Henry Morley, and W. H. Wills. "In and Out of Jail." *Household Words*. No. 164. 14 May 1853: 241-45.

Dickens, Charles, and W. H. Wills. "Idiots." *Household Words*. No. 167. 4 June 1853: 313-17.

———. "The Metropolitan Protectives." *Household Words*. No. 57. 26 Apr. 1851: 97-105.

PARLIAMENTARY PAPERS

"First and Second Reports from the Select Committee of the House of Lords on the Present State of the Several Gaols and Houses of Correction in England and Wales with Minutes of Evidence and Appendices." [1835 (438) Vol. 11] *British Parliamentary Papers*. Crime and Punishment. Vol. 3. Shannon: Irish Univ. Press, 1968.

"Report of the Commissioners in Lunacy Relative to the Haydock Lodge Lunatic Asylum." [1847 (147) Vol. 49] *British Parliamentary Papers*. Health: Mental. Vol. 6. Shannon: Irish Univ. Press, 1969.

"Report of the Commissioners of Lunacy as to the State and Management of Bethlehem Hospital." [1852-53 (75) Vol. 49] *British Parliamentary Papers.* Health: Mental. Vol. 6. Shannon: Irish Univ. Press, 1969.

"Report from the Select Committee on Lunatics." [1859] *British Parliamentary Papers.* Health: Mental. Vol. 3. Shannon: Irish Univ. Press, 1968.

"Report from the Select Committees on the State of Pauper Lunatics in the County of Middlesex." [1826-27 (557) Vol. 6] *British Parliamentary Papers.* Health: Mental. Vol. 2. Shannon: Irish Univ. Press, 1968.

SECONDARY SOURCES

Ackroyd, Peter. *Dickens.* New York: HarperCollins, 1990.

Altick, Richard D. *Victorian People and Ideas.* New York: W. W. Norton, 1973.

Bartky, Sandra Lee. "Foucault, Femininity, and the Modernization of Patriarchal Power." In *Feminism and Foucault: Reflections on Resistance.* Ed. by Irene Diamond and Lee Quinby. Boston: Northeastern Univ. Press, 1988. 61-86.

Billington, Sandra. *A Social History of the Fool.* New York: St. Martin's Press, 1984.

———. " 'Suffer Fools Gladly': The Fool in Medieval England and the Play *Mankind.*" In *The Fool and the Trickster: Studies in Honour of Enid Welsford.* Ed. by Paul V. A. Williams. Cambridge: D. S. Brewer, 1979. 36-54.

Bloomfield, Morton W., ed. *In Search of Literary Theory.* Ithaca, NY: Cornell Univ. Press, 1972.

Bordo, Susan. "Anorexia Nervosa: Psychopathology as the Crystallization of Culture." In *Feminism and Foucault: Reflections on Resistance.* Ed. by Irene Diamond and Lee Quinby. Boston: Northeastern Univ. Press, 1988. 87-117.

Briggs, Asa. *Victorian Cities.* New York: Penguin, 1971.

Brooks, Cleanth. "Wordsworth and Human Suffering: Notes on Two Early Poems." In *Sensibility to Romanticism: Essays Presented to Frederick A. Pottle.* Ed. by Frederick W. Hilles and Harold Bloom. New York: Oxford Univ. Press, 1965. 373-87.

Butt, John, and Kathleen Tillotson. *Dickens at Work.* London: Methuen, 1957.

Bynum, William F., Jr. "Rationales for Therapy in British Psychiatry, 1780-1835." In *Madhouses, Mad-Doctors, and Madmen: The Social History of Psychiatry in the Victorian Era.* Ed. by Andrew Scull. London: Athlone Press, 1981. 35-57.

Carey, John. *The Violent Effigy: A Study of Dickens'* Imagination. London: Faber and Faber, 1973.

Carlyle, Thomas. *Chartism. Critical and Miscellaneous Essays.* Vol. 4 of 5. New York: AMS Press, 1969. 118-204.

———. *Sartor Resartus.* Centenary Edition. New York: Scribner's, n.d.

Chesterton, George Laval. "A Prison Anecdote." *Household Words.* No. 47. 15 Feb. 1851: 496-98.

Cobbe, Frances Power. "Criminals, Idiots, Women, and Minors." *Fraser's Magazine,* December 1868: 777-94.

Collins, Philip. *Dickens and Crime.* 2nd ed. London: Macmillan, 1965.

———. *Dickens and Education.* New York: St. Martin's Press, 1963.

Cotsell, Michael. "Politics and Peeling Frescoes: Layard of Ninevah and *Little Dorrit.*" *Dickens Studies Annual* 15 (1986): 181-200.

———. "Nicholas Nickleby: Dickens's First Young Man." *Dickens Quarterly* 5, no. 3 (1988): 118-28.

———. "The Uncommercial Traveller on the Commercial Road: Dickens's East End." Part One. *Dickens Quarterly* 3, no. 2 (1986): 75-83.

———. "The Uncommercial Traveller on the Commercial Road: Dickens's East End." Part Two. *Dickens Quarterly* 3, no. 3 (1986): 115-23.

Crawford, Iain. "Nature . . . Drenched in Blood": *Barnaby Rudge* and Wordsworth's "The Idiot Boy." *Dickens Quarterly* 9, no. 1 (1991): 38-47.

———. "Pip and the Monster: The Joys of Bondage." *Studies in English Language* 28(1988): 625-48.

Culler, Jonathan. *The Pursuit of Signs: Semiotics, Literature, Deconstruction.* Ithaca, NY: Cornell Univ. Press, 1981.

Diamond, Irene, and Lee Quinby, eds. *Feminism and Foucault: Reflections on Resistance.* Boston: Northeastern Univ. Press, 1988.

Dostoevsky, Fyodor. *The Idiot.* Trans. by Constance Garnett. New York: Macmillan, 1951.

Eagleton, Terry. *The Function of Criticism: From the Spectator to Post-Structuralism.* London: Verso, 1984.

Easson, Angus. "Emotion and Gesture in *Nicholas Nickleby.*" *Dickens Quarterly* 5, no. 3 (1988): 136-51.

Feder, Lillian. *Madness in Literature.* Princeton, NJ: Princeton Univ. Press, 1980.

Forster, John. *Life of Charles Dickens.* 1876. New York: Hearst's, n.d.

Foucault, Michel. *Discipline and Punish: The Birth of the Prison.* Trans. by Alan Sheridan. New York: Pantheon, 1977.

———. *The History of Sexuality.* Trans. by Robert Hurley. New York: Pantheon, 1978.

————. *Madness and Civilization, A History of Insanity in the Age of Reason.* Trans. by Richard Howard. New York: Pantheon, 1965.

Friedberg, Joan B. "Alienation and Integration in *Barnaby Rudge.*" *Dickens Studies Newsletter* 11 (1980): 11-15.

Garnham, Alan. *Psycholinguistics: Central Topics.* New York: Methuen, 1985.

Garrett, Peter K. *The Victorian Multiplot Novel.* New Haven: Yale Univ. Press, 1980.

Gates, Barbara. *Victorian Suicide: Mad Crimes and Sad Histories.* Princeton, NJ: Princeton Univ. Press, 1988.

Gier, Nicholas F. *Wittgenstein and Phenomenology: A Comparative Study of the Later Wittgenstein, Husserl, Heidegger, and Merleau-Ponty.* Albany: SUNY Press, 1981.

Gifford, D. J. "Iconographical Notes Toward a Definition of the Medieval Fool." In *The Fool and the Trickster: Studies in Honour of Enid Welsford.* Ed. by Paul V. A. Williams. Cambridge: D. S. Brewer, 1979. 18-35.

Gilbert, Elliot L. " 'In Primal Sympathy': *Great Expectations* and the Secret Life." *Dickens Studies Annual* 11 (1983): 89-113.

Gilbert, Sandra M., and Susan Gubar. *The Madwoman in the Attic: The Woman Writer and the Nineteenth-Century Literary Imagination.* New Haven, CT: Yale Univ. Press, 1979.

Gilmour, Robin. "Between Two Worlds: Aristocracy and Gentility in *Nicholas Nickleby.*" *Dickens Quarterly* 5, no. 3 (1988): 110-18.

Gitter, Elisabeth A. "Laura Bridgman and Little Nell." *Dickens Quarterly* 8, no. 2 (1991): 75-79.

Goldberg, Michael. *Carlyle and Dickens.* Athens: Univ. of Georgia Press, 1972.

Golding, Robert. *Idiolects in Dickens: Major Techniques and Chronological Development.* London: Macmillan, 1985.

Greenstein, Michael. "Liminality in *Little Dorrit.*" *Dickens Quarterly* 7, no. 2 (1990): 275-83.

Grove, Thelma. "Barnaby Rudge: A Case Study in Autism." *Dickensian* Autumn (1987): 139-48.

Heidegger, Martin. *On the Way to Language.* Trans. by P. D. Hertz. New York: Harper & Row, 1971.

Henkle, Roger B. "New Work in the Study of Literature and Society: Applications for the Analysis of Nineteenth-Century British Fiction." *Dickens Studies Annual* 14 (1985): 337-57.

Herst, Beth F. "*Nicholas Nickleby* and the Ideas of the Hero." *Dickens Quarterly* 5, no. 3 (1988): 128-36.

Hollington, Michael. *Dickens and the Grotesque.* London: Croom Helm, 1984.

————. "Monstrous Faces: Physiognomy in *Barnaby Rudge.*" *Dickens Quarterly* 9, no. 1 (1991): 6-14.

Horton, Susan. *Interpreting Interpreting: Interpreting Dickens*'s Dombey. Baltimore: Johns Hopkins Univ. Press, 1979.

House, Humphry. *The Dickens World.* 2nd ed. Oxford: Oxford Univ. Press, 1942.

Howitt, Anna Mary. "A Chapter of Models." *Household Words.* No. 65. 21 June 1851: 298-301.

Hoy, David Couzens, ed. *Foucault: A Critical Reader.* Oxford: Blackwell, 1986.

Johnson, Edgar. *Charles Dickens: His Tragedy and Triumph.* 2 vols. New York: Simon and Schuster, 1952.

Kaplan, Fred. *Dickens: A Biography.* New York: William Morrow & Co., 1988.

———. *Sacred Tears: Sentimentality in Victorian Literature.* Princeton, NJ: Princeton Univ. Press, 1987.

Keyte J. M., and M. L. Robinson. "Mr. Dick the Schizophrenic." *Dickensian* 16 (1980): 37-39.

Larson, Janet. "The Arts in These Latter Days: Carlylean Prophecy in *Little Dorrit.*" *Dickens Studies Annual* 8 (1980): 139-96.

———. "Designed to Tell: The Shape of Language in Dickens' *Little Dorrit.*" Ph.D. diss., Northwestern University, 1975.

———. *Dickens and the Broken Scripture.* Athens: Univ. of Georgia Press, 1985.

Lindsay, Jack. "Barnaby Rudge." In *Dickens and the Twentieth Century.* Ed. by John Gross and Gabriel Pearson. Toronto: Univ. of Toronto Press, 1962. 91-106.

Lohrli, Anne. *Household Words: A Weekly Journal 1850-1859 Conducted by Charles Dickens.* Toronto: Univ. of Toronto Press, 1973.

Lukacs, Georg. *The Theory of the Novel.* 1920. Trans. by Anna Bostock. Cambridge, MA: MIT Press, 1971.

Manheim, Leonard. "Dickens' Fools and Madmen." *Dickens Studies Annual* 2 (1972): 69-97.

MacKay, Carol Hanbery. "The Melodramatic Impulse in *Nicholas Nickleby.*" *Dickens Quarterly* 5, no. 3 (1988): 152-61.

Mahon, Michael G. *Foucault's Nietzschean Genealogy: A Study of Michel Foucault's Nietzschean Problematic, 1961-1975.* Albany: SUNY Press, 1992.

Marcus, Steven. *Dickens: From Pickwick to Dombey.* New York: Basic Books, 1965.

Martineau, Harriet. "Deaf Mutes." *Household Words.* No. 209. 25 March 1854: 134-38.

———. "Idiots Again." *Household Words.* No. 212. 15 April 1854: 197-200.

McGowan, John P. "Mystery and History in *Barnaby Rudge.*" *Dickens Studies Annual* 9 (1981): 33-52.

McMaster, Juliet. " 'Better to Be Silly': From Vision to Reality in *Barnaby Rudge*." *Dickens Studies Annual* 13 (1984): 1-17.

———. *Dickens the Designer*. Totawa, NJ: Barnes and Noble, 1987.

Meckier, Jerome. "Dickens and King Lear: A Myth for Victorian England." *South Atlantic Quarterly* Winter (1971): 75-90.

———. *Hidden Rivalries in Victorian Fiction: Dickens, Realism and Revaluation*. Lexington: Univ. of Kentucky Press, 1987.

Metz, Nancy Aycock. "The Blighted Tree and the Book of Fate: Female Models of Storytelling in *Little Dorrit*." *Dickens Studies Annual* 18 (1989): 221-41.

Miller, D. A. *The Novel and the Police*. Berkeley: Univ. of California Press, 1988.

Miller, J. Hillis. *Charles Dickens: The World of His Novels*. Cambridge, MA: Harvard Univ. Press, 1965.

———. *The Disappearance of God*. Oxford: Oxford Univ. Press, 1963.

Miller, Robin Fever. *Dostoevsky and the Idiot*. Cambridge, MA: Harvard Univ. Press, 1981.

Morley, Henry. "A Great Idea." *Household Words*. No. 126. 21 August 1852: 546-48.

Morley, Henry and Richard Oliver. "The Treatment of the Insane." Part 2. *Household Words*. No. 115. 5 June 1852: 270-73.

Moynahan, Julian. "Dealings with the Firm of Dombey and Son: Firmness versus Wetness." In *Dickens and the Twentieth Century*. Ed. by John Gross and Gabriel Pearson. Toronto: Univ. of Toronto Press, 1962. 121-31.

Newman, S. J. "*Barnaby Rudge*: Dickens and Scott." In *Literature of the Romantic Period 1750-1850*. Ed. by R. T. Davies and B. G. Beatty. Liverpool: Liverpool Univ. Press, 1976. 171-88.

———. *Dickens at Play*. New York: St. Martin's Press, 1981.

Oliver, Richard. "The Treatment of the Insane." *Household Words*. No. 76. 6 Sept. 1851: 572-76; 5 June 1852: 270-73.

Priestley, Philip. *Victorian Prison Lives; English Prison Biography 1830-1914*. London: Methuen, 1985.

Pykett, Lyn. "*Dombey and Son*: A Sentimental Family Romance." *Studies in the Novel* 19 (1987): 16-30.

Rabinow, Paul, ed. *The Foucault Reader*. New York: Pantheon Books, 1984.

Rice, Thomas. "*Barnaby Rudge*: A Vade Mecum for the Theme of Domestic Government in Dickens." *Dickens Studies Annual* 7 (1978): 81-102.

Roberts, Bette B. "Travel Versus Imprisonment: The 'Fellow Travellers' in *Little Dorrit*." *Dickens Studies Newsletter* 13, no. 4 (1982): 109-12.

Rosenberg, Brian. "Reading the World: Visual Imagination in Dickens and Ruskin." *The Arnoldian* 11, no. 1 (1984): 5-13.

Rothburn, Robert Charles. "Dickens' Periodical Essays and Their Relationships to the Novels." Ph.D. diss., University of Minnesota, 1957.

Salusinszky, Imre, ed. *Criticism in Society.* New York: Methuen, 1987.

Sawicki, Jana. *Disciplining Foucault: Feminism, Power, and the Body.* New York: Routledge, 1991.

———. "Identity Politics and Sexual Freedom: Foucault and Feminism." In *Feminism and Foucault: Reflections on Resistance.* Ed. by Irene Diamond and Lee Quinby. Boston: Northeastern Univ. Press, 1988.

Schuster, Charles I. "Dickens and the Language of Alienation." *English Language Notes* 16 (1978): 117-28.

Schwarzbach, F. S. "Dickens and Carlyle Again: A Note on an Early Influence." *Dickensian* 73 (1977): 149-53.

Scott, Sir Walter. *The Heart of Midlothian.* Intro. by David Daiches. 1948. New York: Holt, Rinehart and Winston, 1962.

Scull, Andrew, ed. *Madhouses, Mad-Doctors, and Madmen: The Social History of Psychiatry in the Victorian Era.* London: Athlone Press, 1981.

———. "The Social History of Psychiatry in the Victorian Era." In *Madhouses, Mad-Doctors, and Madmen: The Social History of Psychiatry in the Victorian Era.* London: Athlone Press, 1981. 5-32.

———. "Moral Treatment Reconsidered: Some Sociological Comments on an Episode in the History of British Psychiatry." In *Madhouses, Mad-Doctors, and Madmen: The Social History of Psychiatry in the Victorian Era.* London: Athlone Press, 1981. 105-18.

Shakespeare, William. *As You Like It.* Riverside edition. Boston: Houghton Mifflin, 1974.

———. *Hamlet.* Riverside edition. Boston: Houghton Mifflin, 1974.

———. *King Lear.* Riverside edition. Boston: Houghton Mifflin, 1974.

———. *Twelfth Night.* Riverside edition. Boston: Houghton Mifflin, 1974.

Shatto, Susan. "Miss Havisham and Mr. Mopes the Hermit: Dickens and the Mentally Ill." Part I. *Dickens Quarterly* 2, no. 2 (1985): 43-50.

———. "Miss Havisham and Mr. Mopes the Hermit: Dickens and the Mentally Ill." Part 2. *Dickens Quarterly* 2, no. 3 (1985): 79-84.

Showalter, Elaine. "Guilt, Authority, and the Shadows of *Little Dorrit.*" *Nineteenth-Century Fiction* 34 (1979): 36-39.

———. "Victorian Women and Insanity." In *Madhouses, Mad-Doctors, and Madmen: The Social History of Psychiatry in the Victorian Era.* Ed. by Andrew Scull. London: Athlone Press, 1981. 313-36.

Slater, Michael. *Dickens and Women.* Stanford, CA: Stanford Univ. Press, 1983.

Smart, Barry. *Foucault, Marxism and Critique.* Boston: Routledge & Kegan Paul, 1983.

Stone, Harry. *Dickens and the Invisible World*. Bloomington: Indiana Univ. Press, 1979.

——. *Charles Dickens' Uncollected Writings from Household Words 1850-1859*. Vol. 2. Bloomington: Indiana Univ. Press, 1968.

Sturrock, Jonathan, ed. *Structuralism and Since: From Levi-Strauss to Derrida*. Oxford: Oxford Univ. Press, 1979.

Tambling, Jeremy. "Prison-bound: Dickens and Foucault." *Essays in Criticism* 36, no. 1 (1986): 11-31.

Tillotson, Kathleen. "Dombey and Son." In *Dickens: A Collection of Critical Essays*. Twentieth Century Views. Ed. by Martin Price. Englewood Cliffs, NJ: Prentice-Hall, 1967. 115-134.

——. *Novels of the Eighteen-Forties*. Oxford: Clarendon Press, 1954.

Trilling, Lionel. "Little Dorrit." In *Dickens: A Collection of Essays*. Ed. by Martin Price. Englewood Cliffs, NJ: Prentice-Hall, 1967. 147-57.

Walton, John. "The Treatment of Pauper Lunatics in Victorian England: The Case of Lancaster Asylum, 1816-1870." In *Madhouses, Mad-Doctors, and Madmen: The Social History of Psychiatry in the Victorian Era*. Ed. by Andrew Scull. London: Athlone Press, 1981. 166-97.

Welsford, Enid. *The Fool: His Social and Literary History*. 1935. Gloucester, MA: Peter Smith, 1966.

Williams, Paul V. A., ed. *The Fool and the Trickster: Studies in Honour of Enid Welsford*. Cambridge: D. S. Brewer, 1979.

Wills, W. H. "The Great Penal Experiments." *Household Words*. No. 11. 8 June 1850: 250-53.

Wilson, Edmund. "Dickens: The Two Scrooges." *The Wound and the Bow*. New York: Oxford Univ. Press, 1947. 17-47.

Wittgenstein, Ludwig Josef Johann. *Vermischte Bemerkungen*. Frankfurt: Suhrkamp, 1977.

Wordsworth, William. *The Poetical Works of Wordsworth*. Cambridge Edition. Boston: Houghton Mifflin, 1982.

INDEX